THE SILVER BULLETS OF COMMERCIAL NEGOTIATION

This book empowers you to immediately grasp the opportunities that present themselves in international commercial negotiation, and to be able to create and maintain positive, mutually beneficial relationships with other parties that are long lasting and productive.

International commercial negotiations are a vital element of today's business world. But how do you conduct them successfully? And how well trained, prepared and knowledgeable are those conducting the negotiation? What makes this book different is that it encapsulates the core 'need to know' elements of negotiation that can make or break a deal. It is written to be user-friendly and an easy read – it offers simple advice that will be immediately useful to the commercial negotiator and makes many complicated issues easily understandable. 'Silver Bullets' are provided, distilling the critical factors that have significant implications for the negotiated outcome.

This book has been written with the experienced business professional who is engaged within commercial negotiations in mind. It provides new insight into how to add value in terms of negotiation skills and operational efficiency. The book has been deliberately written in a non-technical, easy-to-read style that will have broad appeal.

Christopher Lennon is the Director of Stone Falcon Corporate and Legal Consulting Ltd. An International Commercial Arbitrator and Mediator, he was empanelled at the Asian International Arbitration Centre (AIAC), specialising in project-related disputes. He has advised a number of governments as well as many business organisations on contractual/negotiating strategies and tactics, and has taught commercial negotiation internationally for nearly 14 years to professional audiences.

"This is a very readable insight into the nuanced world of negotiation. Chris Lennon expertly navigates its complexities and provides useful guidance and aide-memoire for those involved."

Mark Thompson, *Founder, Epeus Ltd*

"In this book, Chris Lennon gives a balanced view on the various approaches and skill sets required during the negotiation process. His ability to focus on the key components plus the cultural and behavioural considerations that influence the way that a value proposition is both given and received, will have the reader identifying with their own personal experiences of perceived successes and failures and will be an excellent reference point for anyone looking to participate in the negotiation process on either a personal or business level."

Steve Johnson, *MSc, FCIPS Chartered Ex Dip, FCILT, Group Commercial Director, TEXO*

"Chris examines the topic of negotiation from various practical angles based on his many years of 'in the field' experience advising clients."

Mark Tudor, *Regional Counsel at BW Offshore Singapore Pte Ltd*

"Lennon teaches that power and self-interest are key drivers on both sides of any negotiation. He highlights that it is vital at the outset to assess your own negotiating power, and just as important, assess the negotiating power of the other side. Look for the points where the self-interest of the parties coincides and direct your negotiation accordingly. These are lessons we all need to 'relearn' before we start every new negotiation."

Uisdean Vass, *Managing Director, VassPetro Limited*

"An informative read with a pragmatic approach to negotiating; always with the 'end result' in mind, an 'aide memoire' for the seasoned negotiator and a definitive road map for those wishing to learn more about commercial negotiation."

Simon James, *CEng MEI, CMgr FCMI, LLM, MSc, Managing Director, Capability James Ltd*

"Christopher Lennon is a master negotiator, as demonstrated in his 'Silver Bullets'. Readers of all backgrounds and disciplines will gain an advantage in their negotiating prowess, leading the reader to success. Mr. Lennon has not only made the negotiating process crystal clear, but he has also evolved it with his coined terms such as 'Psychic Armour'. Commercial negotiation is truly an art form, very much like the art of winemaking, where the negotiator must equip himself with the arsenal of tools necessary to navigate the perilous line between success and failure, whether it be across the boardroom table or in the winery business. This is precisely what Chris has demonstrated in this new book, resulting in an enjoyable and informative read."

Dominic Burke, *Head Winemaker, Salvatore Vineyards, Arizona, USA*

"This book will serve as a practical and realistic guide through the demanding and unpredictable art of negotiation. Chris Lennon uses real life examples of strategies and tactics used to achieve acceptable goals and objectives. He achieves this keeping the reader informed of the many pitfalls and risks that can confront the practitioner. A very effective refresher for the experienced negotiator and a must read for the those new to the art."

George Clark, *Sales & Commercial Support Director, Oilfield Service*

"One of the things our own students always valued about Chris's teaching was how it was rooted in his own practical experience, and another thing was his own engaging style of delivery. It is good to see that both are very much to the fore in this new volume from Chris, which will no doubt be a popular and accessible text, which his readership will find rewarding."

Dr Paul Davidson, *School of Engineering, University of Aberdeen*

"I have known Christopher Lennon for more than 30 years and find him very observant, analytical and able to learn from his experience. He applies his mind to every situation and walks away from such a wiser and more capable man. Clearly the author has extensive experience in 'real' negotiations, and has most certainly learned from those. Most importantly, he fully comprehends the fact that one does not 'see' with your eyes only, and not 'hear' with only the ears. As an officer in the SA Army, through turbulent times, and in negotiations with peers, senior command, junior subordinates and civilians in labour disputes, I personally experienced many of the situations he refers to and on many levels, from the strategic to the tactical. In retrospect, I wish I had had the opportunity to study his lessons beforehand. I could certainly have benefited from those. His wisdom and sound approach rings true. I can really recommend this work to any manager or negotiator in any setting, on any level."

Brigadier Genl (Ret) André Retief, *Former General Officer Commanding South African Army Armour Formation, Pretoria, South Africa*

"In this book, I believe that Lennon has managed to encapsulate the very essence of both the negotiation process and its component parts. I found that many concepts and intangible elements were expressed effortlessly, but in such a way that the read was enjoyable and easily understood. I believe that this book will be very useful to those of us engaged within commercial negotiations, in terms of gaining a new perspective and/or some new, value-adding ideas to put into practice."

Jonathan Boud, *Managing Director, SALT Ltd*

"*The Silver Bullets of Commercial Negotiation* is clearly written and understandable. Straight to the point where organizations should aim their strategies in negotiations. Communication is key in the context to align strategy and operation. This should also be the case with regard to change. The external stakeholder/customer should also be aware of the direction. The understanding of culture and values when going international is very important and well addressed."

Elfried Paulina, *Strategic Manager, Curoil, Curacao (Ret.)*

"A useful guide for anyone preparing to conduct a commercial negotiation, full of practical tips and sage advice. Examines the pros and cons of different strategic approaches, with a healthy reminder how to keep self interest in check to secure a lasting deal."

Tim Hardy, *Managing Director, Hardy ADR Consultants Ltd*

"As in his first book *The Silver Bullets of Project Management*, this book is yet again full of practical experiential learning and 'ready to use' advice. Whilst any negotiation process is essentially based on what is known between the parties, a most interesting—if not alarming—aspect is what is unknown between the negotiating parties. In this regard the concepts of deception, misdirection, outright lying and half-truths may be at play in some shape or form. Whilst deception may be deliberate during negotiations, (one party deliberately wants to mislead the counterparty), it may also be 'by pure fluke.' One of the parties may opportunistically use information that was accidently leaked to devise shrewd and powerful counter arguments during the process. In this regard, the author has very practical and valid advice that all negotiators should be on the lookout for and be actively practicing. Truly some very practical insight to detect and manage deception during the negotiation process. A must-read for any negotiator."

Nic Loubser, *Business Strategist, Project Director, KMC Value Creation*

"All who are interested in the subject of power relationships in negotiation must engage with the scintillating ideas in this book based on real world examples from Chris Lennon, a boundary-crossing professional."

Philip TN Koh, *Adjunct Professor, University Malaya; Senior Partner and Corporate & Dispute Resolution Lawyer*

"This is a practical guide to negotiation, written by an experienced and well-qualified negotiator. It is also deeply informed and anything but dry reading."

Dr. JD Lamb, *School of Business, University of Aberdeen*

"This book is a detailed and thoughtful insight into the world of negotiation written by someone with an unrivalled depth of knowledge in the complex world of global energy negotiations, and the informative nature of the book's construction lends its content to many other situations in industry, commerce and one's personal life."

Derek Donald, *Director, George Donald Ltd*

THE SILVER BULLETS OF COMMERCIAL NEGOTIATION

STRATEGIES AND TACTICS

Christopher Lennon

Routledge
Taylor & Francis Group
LONDON AND NEW YORK

Cover image: scanrail

First published 2022
by Routledge
4 Park Square, Milton Park, Abingdon, Oxon OX14 4RN

and by Routledge
605 Third Avenue, New York, NY 10158

Routledge is an imprint of the Taylor & Francis Group, an informa business

British Library Cataloguing-in-Publication Data
A catalogue record for this book is available from the British Library

Library of Congress Cataloging-in-Publication Data
Names: Lennon, Christopher, 1967– author.
Title: The silver bullets of commercial negotiation : strategies and tactics / Christopher Lennon.
Description: Milton Park, Abingdon, Oxon; New York, NY : Routledge, 2022. | Includes index.
Identifiers: LCCN 2021057444 (print) | LCCN 2021057445 (ebook)
Subjects: LCSH: Negotiation in business.
Classification: LCC HD58.6.L466 2022 (print) | LCC HD58.6 (ebook) | DDC 658.4/052—dc23/eng/20211208
LC record available at https://lccn.loc.gov/2021057444
LC ebook record available at https://lccn.loc.gov/2021057445

ISBN: 978-1-032-20474-1 (hbk)
ISBN: 978-1-032-20475-8 (pbk)
ISBN: 978-1-003-26372-2 (ebk)

DOI: 10.4324/9781003263722

Typeset in Bembo
by codeMantra

CONTENTS

1

INTRODUCTION

Traditionally, negotiation was viewed as an adversarial process – it was you against them and winner take all. In some circumstances, this may well still be the case. However, this is an outdated and outmoded approach or methodology. In the author's opinion, the fundamental crux of business should be the creation of sustainable, mutually beneficial relationships that endure over long periods of time – bringing an 'added value' to all parties concerned. I wrote this book based on my experience; having come to the conclusion that although there are a great many books out there on the subject, none of them seemed (to me) to be quite what I was looking for. I was searching for a deeper understanding of human interactions and diversity and how the 'negotiation interface' and the people involved behaved. I wanted to be able to then harness this understanding across nearly any situation that I might find myself in and know what to do and how to act. In short, I wanted to be prepared.

The very essence of the negotiation problem is of course that of uncertainty. No two negotiations, even if negotiating the same subject matter or deal, can or ever will be the same as there are a legion of factors and implications, environmental aspects and of course human foibles. What has to be added to this rather (sometimes) explosive and dynamic mix is the fact that human decision-making (or indeed a human being) is not always rational. This therefore makes it unpredictable in the extreme.

The author recalls a time when he was asked by the MD of a company to evaluate two tender documents for a contract. They were both pretty similar, except that one of the offers was about $500,000 more than the other. We met for lunch. I gave my

DOI: 10.4324/9781003263722-1

opinion; although the more expensive bid provided for a slightly higher quality of materials, it was only a marginal difference and certainly did not justify the price differential. I recommended the cheaper bid was the better one – in my opinion. The MD thought for a moment, nodded and then said that he was going to accept the higher bid. Unperturbed – as I had been hired to provide an opinion, I had done so and knew that my invoice would be settled – I sat back and regarded him for a moment. I asked him why he was going to choose the more expensive bid. He told me that many years previously, the other vendor had stolen his girlfriend and there was no way that he was ever going to give this company any work – period. I'm not normally surprised by much, but that display of irrationality surprised me. It is factors such as these that you cannot know or will never anticipate that create both the complexity and mysticism of negotiation – and, as described above, are (or can be) factors of significant impact.

Another problem that we all face in interacting with others is that we are evolutionarily hardwired to make opinions very quickly about the person or people sitting across the table from us. This is fine and although the old maxim 'you only get one chance to make a first impression' carries a lot of weight, unfortunately this first impression more often than not proves to be wrong. This therefore has the potential to place you at an immediate disadvantage relevant to the other parties, regardless of whatever opinions onerous or otherwise that they may have formed about you. So, we can see that before anything at all has started, and as we are all engaged within the opening pleasantries and sizing each other up, we are all beginning from a skewed viewpoint.

This is further compounded by the fact that all of us (either consciously or subconsciously) begin from a position of self-interest (albeit from the organisational as opposed to the individual perspective or a combination of both). It is an instinctive thought process that attempts to make an assessment as to how a particular situation can be of benefit to the individual in question, that is, 'what's in it for me?' This is discussed later on in more depth.

One of the commonest human follies is the failure to not 'see' what is actually in front of you. Negotiation as a subject is as broad as the sky and as deep as the ocean; the interactive processes across nearly infinite combinations of interface make it a subject that is difficult at best to grasp in all of its possible complexities. The sheer quantum nature of these possibilities can be daunting, at best. This is mitigated, however, to a certain extent by the fact that commercial negotiations tend to have a purpose; there is a reason that these particular parties are facing one another across the negotiation table – they want something from one another. The author would suggest that having a clear understanding of what is pertinent and relevant to the negotiation at hand would serve very well in keeping the process on track and in focus. All too often, time and energy become devoted to peripheral issues. Every negotiation has a core issue or issues; this is where the focus must be directed and concentrated, otherwise valuable time is lost. I am very fond of saying that time is the most precious resource and when you lose it, it is gone forever and you can never have it back.

The author believes that negotiators have to possess a certain set of traits in order to be successful and that the successful negotiator is quite different from a lot of other people as a result of these character traits. Paramount among these has to be the ability to effectively make decisions. If we consider the discussion thus far, it is obvious that decision-making within a negotiation setting is going to be significant. It could drive the process towards either success or failure. There is a need to make decisions objectively – emotions must be removed; there is no place for the subjective on the analysis of established hard facts and cold data. It is inevitable that some of these decisions will be 'tough' or difficult to make. I think that if the situation arises where such decisions must be made, then the negotiator cannot and indeed must not flinch from his or her duty in order to achieve the required result. We will take a more in-depth look at psychological and personality traits as to how they shape both behaviour and decision-making processes in a later chapter.

People aside, the environment of the negotiation contains a plethora of influencing aspects that will interact on those involved. Often the place where a negotiation is set to happen can have many subtle and sublime purposes – designed to distract or influence mood and opinion. Vision is the primary sense of humans; therefore, colour, lighting, location and set-up (lay out) are all factors that will have an immediate (more often than not) subconscious impact upon someone walking into the room. Take it from me; a lot of thought goes into these details, especially if the negotiation in question is high stakes. As mentioned, where the negotiation is going to occur has great significance: Is it on home territory? Neutral ground? Or on the home ground of the other party? This is very important. All of these issues will be discussed in detail in a later chapter.

In the author's opinion, when it comes to complex, commercial agreements and the negotiation of them, there is never a truer adage than that of 'The Devil is in the details.' What do I mean? Well, obviously the bigger the deal, the more intricate and complex it's going to be. But that's obvious. What I am referring to here is the question of preparation and readiness. The author knows many a negotiator who found themselves the recipient of a nasty surprise and it wasn't from something unexpected like the kind of factors discussed thus far. It was from overlooking or not 'seeing' or recognising something for what it was and having a strategy in place, that is, being caught with one's figurative pants down. In this book, there is quite a lot of focus on the idea of planning and preparing for a negotiation. I have included a few templates and other processes to help the reader get better ready for what lies ahead. I would suggest that there is no excuse for being caught unawares by something that you should have been fully cognisant of, if it happens – simply, you haven't done your homework in getting prepared.

I believe that any negotiator should view the negotiation from two perspectives, and if I may, I'd like to borrow two military adages here. First, the 'general's view' from the top of the high ground (sometimes in contemporary parlance referred to as the 'helicopter view'). As it would suggest, those commanding the action need to be able to see the entire picture in order to act and react as required. Second, knowing how to 'fight in the trenches.' This is where it's up close, dirty and personal. This is the sharp end where all the action is. So, we could paraphrase these two perspectives into the strategic and tactical elements and aspects of the negotiation at hand. Another useful way of considering this is to think macro-level and micro-level. The strategy informs and guides the action and the tactical performs the execution. The key to success here lies within the providence of common sense. After you've gone to all the trouble to formulate your strategy and how you are going to execute and implement it (tactics), you need to have some form of monitoring and control mechanism in place. This will allow you (and the team if applicable) to review and measure the actual against the expected and ideal during break times or at end of the day (should the negotiation be a protracted endeavour), thus providing the opportunity to bring something back on track that might be a deviation from where you want to be or simply to regain control over something that might be becoming a little errant (perhaps before the other side realises). It must be remembered that all plans are of a limited use for a limited time. You must monitor, control and review what's happening as often as is realistically possible and I would definitely suggest a team review meeting back at the hotel every night if involved in a complex, drawn out process. This is discussed fully in several places later in the book. To reinforce the above discussion to quantify and qualify what's being said, the author suggests that discipline is of paramount importance – discipline in conduct (i.e. not giving anything away emotively when events take a dramatic turn), discipline in following the strategy and executing it, discipline in recognising the vitality of flexibility and being able to adapt and discipline towards achieving what you came for.

Furthermore, when having these sorts of progress meetings, the author thinks that a time for honest self-assessment in reviewing the performance of the day is very important. If you are operating solo, then you should consider your conduct throughout the events of the day and ask yourself what went well, what could've been better and what didn't go well. This is equally applicable to a team-based scenario. Remember though that this is not as easy as it sounds. In the team setting, it is important to understand that this is not a negative process. This is not about assigning blame and pointing fingers. Rather (especially if you are back at the table the following day), this is about tightening up weaknesses in performance regardless of what and who might be responsible. It is about refreshing and resetting the way forward. It might be about damage mitigation or it might be that you (or the team) can amend your strategy to deal with an emergent opportunity. This will be discussed at length in a later chapter.

2

THE CRITICAL CHOICE

Compete or Co-operate?

Forget all of the myriad of articles that espouse 'touching feely,' 'warm' and 'fuzzy' approaches to negotiation. It is a serious business and, as stated earlier, one that both or all parties are wanting something from that personally benefits them for whatever reason. In essence, there are only three possible ways that a negotiation can be approached. It can be from a competitive perspective, it can be from a co-operative perspective or it may be that there is a combination of both of these elements relative to different parts or stages of the process. This latter point is mentioned at the end of the introduction when talking about emergent opportunities. It may be that some form of change or turn of events dictates a revision of the strategy and execution of your plan.

First, let's examine the co-operative dimension of negotiation. There are several factors that might underpin this approach and all of them are both valid and worthwhile, where there is a power inequality between the parties. In this instance, it is almost certain that the weaker party will be dictated to and acquiesces to the terms and conditions as laid out by the stronger party. The weaker party in these circumstances has little choice but to be co-operative if they wish to do business. There is an interesting dynamic involved with market power distribution. The stronger party might be a big international venture, whilst the weaker party is a smaller organisation; so in the course of normal business, the relationship is likely to be as described above. The author recalls giving a negotiation seminar to a group of senior commercial negotiators and asking the question right at the start: 'So tell me, how do you negotiate?' There were a

DOI: 10.4324/9781003263722-2

few rueful smiles around the room, and then one of the most senior people present said:

> It's very easy actually – we give them our terms and conditions, they take them, thank us and then give us their terms and conditions. Then they tell us that if we wish to do business with them – it is on the basis of their T&C's – non-negotiable – take it or leave it, so we have no choice but to take it.

It is not always the case that the bigger company (in the example above, the smaller company was actually quite a big international entity; it was just small compared to the other party) holds all the cards though. I can recall a company that was the owner of a specific proprietary technology that was very much in demand as it saved the other organisations a lot of money operationally (we're talking oil and gas industry here). The scenario above was reversed completely. If the larger organisations wished to utilise the technology of the smaller company, then they paid what was asked; there was no debate.

Whilst this might seem fairly intractable to the reader, it is a scenario that commonly plays out in meeting and board rooms on a daily basis around the world. There is one aspect that is perhaps overlooked with this attitude – that of longer-term relationships. Decision makers and organisational negotiators are aware of this dimension to corporate dealings, evidenced, for example, by the increasing advent of vendor partnering and supply chain finance initiatives.

What might become apparent to the reader is that co-operation may well be better termed as 'forced co-operation,' in light of the examples given above. There will be times when there is no magical solution, no silver bullet to save the day where you have little choice or any real room to manoeuvre. When you find yourself in this position, it is of extreme importance that you have a termination or 'walk away' point. This is where you will leave the table – the negotiation process is concluded without a result. It is fair to say that sometimes having a 'point of no return' where you are prepared to walk away can in itself be a lever that will prompt the other party to perhaps offer some form of concession, to break their rigidity and stance. In poker parlance, you have called their bluff, whether intentionally or not.

Whether or not the co-operative scenarios above are played out in this way (as opposed to true co-operation, things like joint venture [JV] negotiations), one element that has to be evaluated is what you see the outcome scenario to look like. To the author, scenario generation on the back of the due diligence process is of vital importance as it allows a modicum of a 'view of what might be.' We'll discuss this in a later chapter.

Ultimately, there is an individual somewhere who will have the final say. Often, the path chosen will be strongly influenced by the organisations' (or decision makers') attitude to risk and what their overarching risk strategy might be that is required to be implemented. The author would suggest that from this overarching perspective, there are five broad generic strategies that are utilised either in isolation to one another or perhaps selected on the basis of the issue or negotiation at hand.

First, there is the strategy of 'remove.' What this tells us is that a risk of some sort exists and has been identified by the organisation/individual. There does not appear to be any effective risk mitigation option other than to remove it. From the business perspective, this might well be represented by a decision to outsource something (i.e. no longer attempt to maintain or control it internally); it may be more cost-effective for it to be managed by specialists who operate exclusively within this particular domain. From the negotiation perspective, it might be a disclosure best not made to the other parties. This might be achieved simply by removing a particular item from the negotiation agenda – taking it 'off the table' discreetly and quietly.

Second (and the author would suggest, very commonly), there is the strategy of reduce or mitigate a risk. Again, the risk has been identified and evaluated and there is action that can be taken to reduce the impact should it manifest. From a corporate perspective, this might be to invest in more specialist training for personnel who are directly involved or, if we consider high value items, investment in security provisions. From the negotiation table perspective, mitigation might well be attempting to diminish the impact of new information, or a significant deviation from the planned agenda or a mistake made (i.e. disclosing something that could now give the counterparty an advantage, a 'slip of the tongue').

Third, the risk strategy might be to retain the risk; the organisation might decide that they are best placed to manage a particular risk through their knowledge and expertise. From the negotiation perspective, this might be reflected as a deliberate tactic – telling the counterparty that you will continue to do 'X' and not to worry, but to attempt to utilise this strategy as a grand gesture that you can capitalise on, perhaps to get those sitting on the opposite side of the table to feel an emotional debt towards you, to perhaps be either compelled or guided into some kind of trade off that is of particular value to you when you had already decided that you would keep this risk (unbeknownst to them).

Fourth, the approach might be to share a particular risk. This strategy is common as it is the basis for much co-operative business deals that are negotiated. In the international oil and gas industry, for instance, JVs are fairly commonplace and standard practice. This is often due to a number of factors such as amount of investment required and the length of time until payback. What has always been of particular interest to the author though is the dark side of JVs, when a seemingly sensible plan such as sharing the risk between parties (and thereby limiting your risk exposure to your particular contribution) actually is the vehicle for other agendas. The most common ones that I can think of almost instantly are gaining access to a new market or territory, having access to infrastructure such as ports and warehousing, or getting your hands on proprietary technology or process. The former two tend to contain less skulduggery but might still be representative of a deliberate or devious manipulation, whilst the latter can often result in disputes, based on the idea that the JV partner who doesn't have the technology or know how in question has entered into the arrangement with the intention of utilising said technology or process far and wide as opposed to being limited to the venture at hand. This is why Contract Law is the most difficult area of law (in the authors view); as if it is not illegal and the parties to the contract agree to be bound by the rights, duties and obligations contained therein, then the possibilities are almost infinite, and if you've signed within the criteria above, then welcome to your new reality!

Lastly, and perhaps the most common sense of the broader risk strategies, is that of avoidance. This might encapsulate known risks but may also prevent unknown risks from manifesting and impacting simply because you're not involved. Quite often, when I am consulting with clients, particularly about potential projects that they may decide to initiate, it is normal for the decision maker to tell me: 'We have selected a number of options – all with different features; advantages and disadvantages (such as timing or returns; payback period; amount of investment required and when required, etc.) and would like your opinion.' Many has been the time when I have remarked to a client that there is another option that they have not considered. This is often met with a frown and a quick skim over the documents in question, inevitably followed by the statement 'I don't think so.' Well, the other option is simply don't bother doing anything at the particular time, thereby avoiding any and all possible consequences. Perhaps the market is unstable, perhaps there is turbulence in FX parities, perhaps a particular geographic location is subject to political unrest and uncertainty, but by waiting, a multitude of problems are solved and annulled or are simply void as they no longer have any relevance whatsoever.

So, if we accept the premise that our basic starting point within a negotiation is to make a determination as to how we are going to approach it (i.e. competitively or co-operatively or some kind of 'hybrid' approach dependent upon the matters at hand), then we need to consider how to go about making this choice in an organised way that is best configured to our desires and needs.

The six factors listed below are the elements to my template for making this choice:

1 Consider and evaluate what the purpose of the negotiation is
2 Clarify your objectives and goals
3 Consider the relationship angle
4 Consider possible outcomes and their ramifications
5 Quantify how much time you have
6 Assess any financial implications associated with your choice (consider preceding discussion on JVs)

Let's take a closer look at each of these factors in turn:

1 Consider and evaluate what the purpose of the negotiation is

The starting question could simply be 'why am I here?' Quite often, people find themselves engaged or involved within situations that might have initially seemed interesting or promising, but evolve into something that perhaps was better left alone in the first instance. A clear way to think of this is to consider the old adage: 'making a deal with the devil' or 'fools rush in where angels fear to tread.' The author would suggest that you take a step back prior to commitment and clearly understand in your own mind why you are going to be engaging in this particular negotiation and understand what your involvement post-process might entail.

2 Clarify your objectives and goals

Once you are sure in your mind as to the reason and justification of a particular course of action, the next logical step is to understand what you want to achieve from the negotiation and how you are going to do this. I always utilise project management parlance at this stage. In a project, 'milestones' or 'stage gates' are common methodologies for marking the progress of a project towards delivery/completion. What I would suggest that is helpful to you, the reader, here is to consider your objectives in this way – as you achieve (or not) each one, a progress marker or a stepping stone that is bringing you a step closer to your goal(s). Objectives as milestones or stage gates are a very structured way of marking progress; in the negotiation sense, you will have a number of objectives that you wish to achieve, for whatever reason. I would suggest that your goal(s) is your end state and achieving it is representative of a culmination of all of the sub-objectives that you were able to close during the process. Don't confuse the two. See the goal(s) as the prize and the objectives as the ladder towards it. I have always found this visualisation both very powerful and useful.

3 Consider the relationship angle

At this juncture, it is possibly a good idea to check by way of reassessment how your thinking thus far is going to be impacted on by this area. Earlier, we discussed the various forms that a negotiation might take (i.e. competitive/co-operative/combo) and the author would suggest that longer-term ambitions and intentions in terms of the counterparty are going to be a significant factor of careful consideration. I made the statement at the start of the book that the best outcome is one where there are no losers (in a perfect world). In order to achieve this (be that your intention for whatever reason), then this is going to be a subject worthy of careful contemplation and consideration prior to any initiation of action.

4 Consider possible outcomes and their ramifications

This is a further link in the chain of reasoning. I hope that the reader understands that this template is representative of a flow not unlike a waterfall – the subcomponents are all linked to the preceding one – forming a holistic picture; there is little point in the author's view of considering these factors in isolation to one another. As we have discussed thus far, it is both reasonable and pragmatic to make an assessment of what chain of events we may or may not set into motion by our actions and decisions around the negotiation table and what the 'end state' might look like. If we perceive things that could go awry or be far from ideal, then the author would suggest that a rethink might be wise.

5 Quantify how much time you have

In my opinion, this is the cornerstone for either success or failure around the negotiation table. It is of vital importance to ensure that you (to the best of your abilities, things being outwith your control aside) do not find yourself under time pressure. As we will see later on, worrying about time is a major catalyst for the onset of stress leading to possible bad or impaired decision-making and irrational behaviour. You must control the usage of the time that you have. As we discussed earlier, you can't really go amiss if you borrow from the project management sphere (discussed in 2 above) and utilise milestones or stage gates. So, this could look like 'Milestone 1 – agreement reached on items 1 through 5 on the agenda no later than noon on day 1.' What this will do is that, apart from increased visibility, it will allow you to track and control where you are and whether or not you are behind, on or ahead of the schedule.

6 Assess any financial implications associated with your choice

Obviously, this is important, and whilst the reader might be wondering if this is a repetition of point (4) above, may I assure you that it is definitely not. I believe that it puts armour on the strength of what you are trying to achieve by thinking about post negotiation state first from a broad perspective (see discussion of point 4 above) that is, strategically and tactically, then to almost overlay the financial information and quantify what any end state might look like from a financial perspective of either cost or gain or some combination thereof.

In addition to the points above, there are some further aspects that we need to be aware of that might dictate how the parties are going to approach the negotiation. As we have established, a negotiation might be co-operative, competitive or some form of mixed model. The author would suggest to the reader that consideration is given to the personality of those who will be conducting the proceedings involved within them. Negotiation is a process that always bears the stamp or mark of those who forged the deal. People are different. Some are naturally competitive and more aggressive, whilst others may seek compromise and wish to engineer a win/win scenario. I feel it is an important part of the preparation process to attempt to understand how the counterparties operate or have operated in the past. The old adage 'a leopard never changes its spots' is a worthy consideration to make here. This will allow you, at the very least, to anticipate likely behaviour and formulate a baseline as to how you think it best to handle this and plan accordingly. Remember that the relative importance (or not) of the issues being negotiated at any particular point within the process (i.e. in terms of money and time at stake) will also impact upon the behaviour of individuals engaged within the negotiation. We will consider how stress impacts and effects behaviour at a later point within the book. The author has alluded to the longer-term, mutually beneficial position several times as being ideal, but would also like to introduce the reader to the counterpoint of this idea. What might the behavioural landscape look like if this is a one-off, short-term deal and there is no interest from any particular party in anything other than attempting to engineer the optimum outcome for their own self-interest (discussed next)? I would suggest that this is likely to be a competitive, if not aggressive, endeavour.

Silver Bullet: There is no universal best approach to commercial negotiations. Be subjective and remember that flexibility and adaptability are easily translated into key advantages when an opportunity arises.

THE PROBLEM OF SELF-INTEREST

As mentioned in the introduction, the author believes that a universal truth about people is that they are ultimately selfish. They may not mean to be. They might not even realise that they are being selfish. They might, however, be driven by their own self-interest. Around the negotiation table, it is important to attempt to get a handle on this phenomenon, to make an assessment of the level of self-interest that is driving (or not) the negotiation process forward. This includes you, not just the counterparties. The self-interest is representative of the 'what's in it for me' syndrome, but this is not necessarily a negative thing (consider the discussion of the previous template). In a commercial negotiation, I believe that there are two dimensions to any self-interest, whether it be tacit or overt. First, it might be representative of ambition, the 'I'm going to make my mark here, be recognised and lauded for my deft skill and control, for the great deal that I am personally going to engineer through my talents and abilities.' I've seen it a thousand times.

Second, it might be organisational self-interest; the negotiators have a mandate representing what the organisation wants to achieve from this process and will therefore bend their will (and hopefully that of the counterparties) towards this end. What the author has always found interesting about the influence of organisational culture on corporate members involved within a negotiation process is just how pervasive and invasive it can be in terms of, for want of a better expression, formatting behaviour. Many successful, large international companies believe that their way is the secret to their competitive advantage, and that some process that is unique to the organisation and how it does things, what are the acceptable behavioural norms and so on are the prescriptions for ultimate success. The author would not agree. The idea of 'cultural imprinting' of employees, that is, the moulding of individuals at the start of their career in the company methodology and approach, obviously has some benefits (hence the relative market position and success of the particular company), but I feel it has many drawbacks as well. Corporate 'clones or drones' who act and function to a prescribed methodology will in many cases lack innovation and creativity and will be confused and disorientated should they find themselves in a situation or environment that does not seem to 'play by the rules.'

Third, and perhaps most commonly, both these dimensions of self-interest may be present and the big question one has to ask oneself is to what degree is this behavioural manifestation deliberate and conscious or simply ingrained and automatic – a result (perhaps) of subconscious conditioning?

The author would suggest that the crux of the self-interest problem is that it might define the expectations and positions of the parties right at the start and possibly throughout the entire negotiation process. This in itself can have an influence on the proceedings as well as the outcome. I would suggest that this stricture or straitjacket already in place could prove to be a significant handicap towards moving to a better or more positive outcome where this could be achieved through compromise and flexibility. Self-interest is often a factor that makes a negotiation more competitive than it perhaps needs to be, as the focus is selfish and the desire to be in control. This, in turn, tends to skew the focus of the negotiation towards more short-term 'now' goals and outcomes, often to the detriment of future, longer-term possibilities.

The author believes that another dangerous dimension of self-interest is that negotiations (like practically every other aspect of business) operate within a resource-constrained environment. Let's stop to consider this for a moment. How are resources constrained? Well, first there's the time factor. I've never heard of a negotiation that had unlimited time within which to achieve some sort of outcome. The people sitting around the table will also have other functions and duties to perform within their organisations. There are stakeholder expectations to be met; these in themselves could be a powerful constraint. There are costs involved; it is quite possible that there is a cap or budget on how much is to be invested within a negotiation prior to the walk away point (discussed later). As negotiation is a dynamic, 'live' activity, it is also important to consider that the constraints that exist are not static and can morph and change (i.e. reduce in impact/fade away/rise in prominence/be new) as the negotiation itself progresses.

The key to effectively handling constraints is to have the ability to make trade-off decisions. This implies being able to compromise or accept a significant change in the negotiation environment (i.e. possibly an emergent opportunity or some significant deviation from the original objectives and goals). The author would suggest that this ability is a critical tool in the negotiator's toolbox. In order to be effective though, the individual in question must have complete clarity as to what level of trade-off autonomy they may have. If we consider our earlier discussion regarding organisational culture and the creation/manufacture of corporate clones and drones, the prescription might be such that an individual sitting at the table is not authorised to deviate from the projected/desired outcomes of the negotiation. This needs to be settled prior to commencement. The author can think of few things that would undermine professionalism and credibility more than having to take a break so that an individual can phone their boss to ask for permission/guidance as to what to do. As no negotiation is a static process, having the credibility and authority to make trade-offs literally grants flexibility, the latitude to move and make live decisions, to roll with the process and attempt to achieve the best possible outcomes.

After considering all of the elements discussed thus far, it is obvious that we face a fundamental choice in how we wish to conduct/interact/behave around the negotiation table. All things aside, deciding how you are going to negotiate is not quite as straightforward as it might first appear to be. Sure, you could simply do some research, examine some facts, build a picture of what you want to do and then turn up and take your chances. Whilst the author is certain that this is not an uncommon approach to commercial negotiations, the aim of this book is to give the reader a set of tools and techniques to be *really* prepared.

I would suggest that there are a number of critical factors that should be examined and considered carefully that will directly inform an individual as to the best way to proceed within a negotiation. Let's examine each of these in turn:

First, it's very important to understand what *type* negotiation is at hand. As mentioned in the introduction, the author believes that there are different *strata* of negotiations and they have different levels of importance, are likely to have different time frames and will be of differing levels of complexity. Figure 2.1 shows what I believe to be the ratio of commonality in terms of the type of negotiations occurring. Remember though that I am talking from the perspective of the negotiation table; of course, physically an operational implementation might be very complex and might be over a long period of time, but this illustrates the point I am making here perfectly – the more complex something is, the more complex the negotiation over it will be. The relative importance to the organisation, its business and future sustainable competitive advantage will determine the level or type of negotiation as per the three classes represented in Figure 2.1.

Second is the issue of time. This raises a number of important questions that we should be asking ourselves, such as: What is the time availability? When is the negotiation scheduled to happen? How long do we estimate our preparation time to be? Have we invested enough time in our due diligence process (fact finding and research)? How much contingency time have we allocated?

Third, it is very important to ensure that the negotiation scope is clear – you know what you are negotiating about and you are certain as to what should not take time at the table (i.e. what is out of scope or not included within the spectrum of issues to be considered).

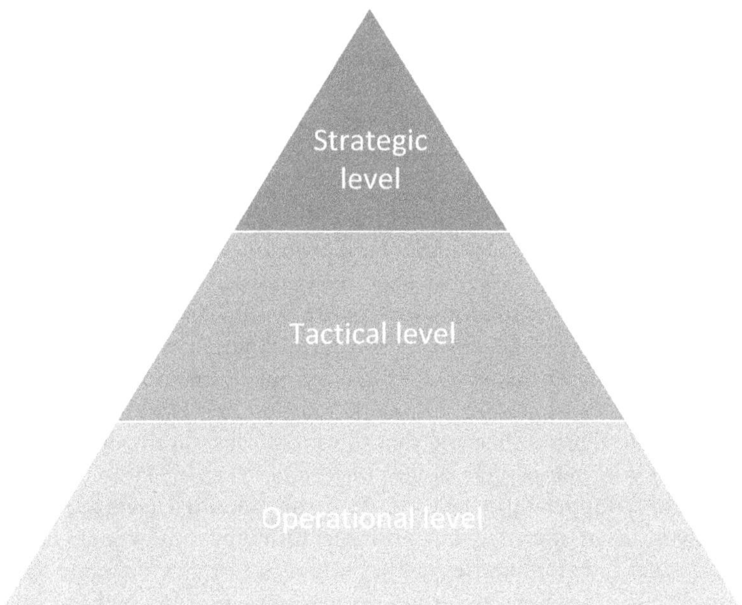

Figure 2.1 The Three Levels of Commercial Negotiation.

Fourth (as discussed above), those who will be conducting the negotiation are empowered to make lateral decisions as the negotiation might evolve and the types of trade-off decisions that might arise have been considered. Additionally, you have identified items that might be subject to 'burn off.' In the author's opinion, the issue of burn off is a very vital one that can make or break a negotiation. By burn off, I mean things that are not really important to you and you are quite willing to sacrifice them in order to achieve some form of *quid pro quo* from the other parties – to show good faith and possibly establish an emotional debt in the minds of the counterparties. However, a word of caution regarding this concept. Many of the things that we have discussed thus far and will discuss further on hinge around the idea of your level of preparedness and knowledge of both the matter at hand and that of the counterparties. In order for burn off to be truly effective, you have to know what the other side wants and what they can give you. Simply put, something that you decide to utilise in this manner might not be very important to you in actuality but could be something that is very important to the other side and vice versa, so it effectively establishes the baseline for the commencement of 'horse trading' which is a fundamental activity within all negotiations.

In the preceding paragraph, I mention the concept of emotional debt. I believe that this is another emotional form of conditioning that is hardwired into our minds subconsciously. If you think about it – how do you feel if someone has done you a favour or gone out of their way for you? Truthfully, you probably feel good about it and if that person was to ask you a favour, you would probably not hesitate to comply, as subconsciously you would feel that you owed them. The author believes that this is no different within the commercial sense and this is where the concept of burn off comes into play. If you can leverage the counterparties' goodwill towards you by granting them something that they want that isn't really important from your perspective or you're willing to sacrifice it in the short term for a longer-term benefit, then this potential leverage could lead you to an advantageous position. Of course, the reader has to realise that the other parties might be applying exactly the same strategy. But this is where it gets interesting, quite possibly by both sides seeming willing to grant concessions and make compromises to each other – even if they are to an extent bluffing through the burn off principle – a final agreement might well be negotiated where both sides are satisfied and believe that they have got a good deal, as they didn't really have to concede anything that they weren't prepared to do in the first instance anyway. I like to think of these situations as 'Smoke and Mirror' negotiations, as in reality each side thinks that they've got a good result; but the level of obfuscation and acting that went into everyone trying to pretend that they were driving or receiving a hard deal and having to consider the weighty issues with appropriate gravitas is, in fact, just a load of bluff all around. Human nature – you've got to love it!

No matter what is happening around the negotiation table, be it positive or negative, one thing that must be kept in mind is that of your exit point or strategy. This is important. Some negotiations can be lengthy and protracted; others don't have such a luxury. This aside, however, never place yourself in an inextricable situation. You must ALWAYS have a point where you are willing to say enough and walk away. In the author's opinion, there are always options even if they, at first, might not be obvious; as mentioned earlier when talking about risk strategies, sometimes simply doing nothing or not getting involved is the option that might make the most sense at a particular time. On the point of identifying or recognising options that may not appear at first as being evident or obvious, I always draw inspiration from the immortal words of Hannibal when he was trying to get his army (and war elephants) over the Alps in the winter to take the war to Rome in Italy. His generals told him it was impossible for a variety of reasons. He is quoted as saying: 'I will either find a way, or make one.' Against seeming impossible odds, the army crossed the mountains in the winter, arriving in Italy itself to progress the war.

The key issue is being able to identify this point. As I have stated several times thus far, negotiation is all about preparation. Therefore, in your planning, you need to have made an assessment of the exit point should it become necessary – what factors or triggers upon manifestation will activate this decision on your part.

Silver Bullet: A clear and concise identification and assessment of likely trigger events that could alter the course of a negotiation negatively should be an essential part of your planning process.

Silver Bullet: There are nexus points within negotiation proceedings that are representative of the need to make critical decisions. These points often represent a crossroad for the parties involved where they must assess both the direction and the likely end state of where the negotiation is heading.

3

THE EFFECTIVE COMMUNICATOR

Managing and Understanding the Verbal/Non-verbal Interface

All possible outcomes from a negotiation process are only achieved through effective and efficient communication. However, I wish to draw the reader's attention to two points: First, most of us are not effective communicators, and second, the spoken word is actually a very minor part of any communication that takes place between humans – believe it or not! There have been numerous research studies within this area and the general consensus appears to be that actual verbal communication (in terms of the words spoken) is less than 10% of the transference of information between different people. If I may return to my first point above, most of us are not efficient communicators and there are quite a few reasons for this, which we will explore in this chapter. It must be remembered that the more complex a negotiation might be and therefore the greater number of interfaces to be managed and the greater number of involved parties (stakeholders), the scope for misunderstanding grows wider. Factor in cross-cultural implications, organisational culture and a potential for lack of clarity in verbal statements and documentation and you have a recipe for possible disaster.

4 KEY RULES FOR EFFECTIVE COMMUNICATION

1 Be concise

If the reader pauses for a moment and considers the rather fraught picture presented at the end of the last paragraph, the realisation should dawn that any sensible starting point from a communicative perspective should be to attempt to prevent or at least mitigate the scope of these problems from occurring.

DOI: 10.4324/9781003263722-3

Cross-culturally, a common approach is to employ translators to overcome the language barriers that might exist. However, this in itself presents issues such as you don't know what the translator is actually saying, so you don't know if they are conveying the actual gist of what you said. This might also be a problem in reverse – how do you know what the counterparty has actually said. Also, this tends to be a rather time-consuming process with the backwards and forwards. The author has had numerous experiences with this and it is often far from ideal. As I mentioned earlier, the art of negotiation is to understand that there is always a core, always some central issues that represent the heart of the matter at hand. Often, this is smothered in 'ground clutter' and peripheral issues that at times lead to a time-wasting divergence and 'hair splitting' that skews the focus away from what is really important and relevant (and sometimes might even be a deliberate strategy).

Silver Bullet: Do not simply be concise in terms of talking and in terms of documentation presentation, but also be concise with focus on the essentials and the management of time.

2 Be aware of what you are saying

The more precise you are in your delivery (in terms of economy and clarity), there is less scope for misunderstandings and confusion manifesting – making the entire process around the negotiation table far more efficient. As already mentioned, fundamentally negotiation is about preparation and planning. Part of this should be to ensure that you and your team are culturally informed. It is often the forgotten element that leads to disaster as an insult or perceived slight might be wholly innocent but won't be forgiven and can derail the process then and there. Another serious aspect to pay careful attention to (and unfortunately occurs far too frequently – the author often wonders how many negotiators might have had a different outcome, if only…) is NEVER get personal. Perhaps easier said than done, but this is the antithesis of professionalism. The people at the other side of the table are not your friends; they are there for the same reason as you – to get a job done. The author was once in a team negotiation situation where things were becoming tense; it was late in the day and people were feeling frayed. Emotion was starting to get the upper hand, as people were beginning to lose focus (non-verbal signs such as shifting around in their seats, tapping pens on the paperwork in front of them, frequent glances at the clock etc.). I think it was generally felt that the constructive process had lost all forward momentum (when we had a team debrief back at the hotel). I was about to suggest a recess until the following day, when suddenly a member of the counterparty looked up belligerently at one of our team and actually called him a liar to his face! My team member reacted badly, jumping to his feet and displaying a very aggressive attitude. Words were exchanged and everyone was on their feet trying to calm the situation down. Truth be told, I was pretty pi**ed off myself at this display. We broke up for the night and returned to our hotel. We sat and discussed this incident. I was also pretty annoyed that a member of what I considered to be a top professional team had lost control of himself reacting to such an outburst. He was quite chagrined and surprised at himself. When I pointed out that this might well have been a deliberate act – a staged set piece to interrupt proceedings – everyone was silently thoughtful. I told the team that they were better trained than that and should always be ready, to flow unemotionally, showing nothing, even if you are surprised and shocked.

Silver Bullet: A true negotiator is always ready. No matter what sudden revelations might occur, they flow unemotionally, showing nothing, no reaction whatsoever they might be feeling inside themselves.

I had a phone call with my opposite number. He was quite apologetic and explained to me that the individual in question was often a difficult person and tended to be rather outspoken, which was often detrimental to a particular situation. He had not wanted him involved with these proceedings, but higher powers had decreed that he had a role to play from a technical perspective. I was told that he had been disciplined and would apologise in the morning and make a concerted effort to conduct himself appropriately around the table. I thanked my counterparty and we ended the call.

Later at the bar, the general consensus from the team was that I had been too lenient and co-operative in accepting a deferred apology (as one put it) and simply letting the matter go. I smiled and shook my head. I explained that we had just secured a number of advantages. First, in the morning, the other team will be a little awkward and embarrassed by their colleague's outburst (it seemed it hadn't been a deliberate ploy). This meant that their focus would be slightly off. Second, the apology would consume time and I instructed everyone to use this time to get their thoughts in order and be ready for the continued execution of our strategy. Third, I had now created an emotional debt with my counterparty (mentioned earlier). I knew that I could push on some things a little harder and he would be more susceptible to acquiesce, subconsciously feeling that he 'owed me one' – perhaps without really even being aware of it.

Silver Bullet: If you are calm and stoic and remain in control of yourself, you may be able to harness negative events for your benefit. The ability to capitalise on negativity and turning it into positivity for your position is worth its weight in gold.

Things transpired the next morning pretty much as expected, and ultimately, we walked away with a positive result, enhanced, I believe, by the sabotage inflicted on the other team by their errant and unprofessional colleague.

3 Understand your audience

In the story above, the author was also executing the third key rule for effective communication – being empathetic. Consider what the path forward might have become had I been aggressive and/or rude. Had I made personal statements about people (discussed above), then the first thing that would have happened is that I would have lost all the advantages that had just been given to us. By allowing my counterparty a positive, professional forum in which to present his case, I was being empathetic. I was demonstrating understanding of his position; I was allowing him to 'save face.' The concept of empathy, of course, is to put yourself into the position of the other party. Try to understand the whats and the whys of their behaviour, motivations and conduct. Empathy is powerful; it most definitely changes outcomes if it is used effectively (and, of course, if you have the ability to be empathic). Empathy is an interesting aspect of human beings and being able to harness this ability is not simply about being able to understand what people say. At the start of this chapter, I mentioned how contemporary research accepted that words themselves were a small part of the total person-to-person communication interface. You can fully develop your empathic abilities (and therefore harness them around the negotiation table) from understanding all the signs and indications coming from other people (i.e. non-verbal questions and behavioural traits). We are all the sum product of our experiences and I utilise this personally whenever I am trying to get into 'someone else's head' to understand them. To borrow from Eastern Philosophy for a moment, I really do believe that to understand someone else, you first have to understand yourself. I have said many times over the years that I would rather find myself facing a male counterpart across the negotiation table rather than a female. The reasons for this are quite a few, but the primary one is the disadvantage you have with attempting to establish rapport. When human beings meet, among the first things they do is (probably subconsciously) seek to establish a common ground. If you and another person discover that you have common interests, this tends to be the first step in establishing some kind of relationship. Across the genders, I believe that there is quite a dichotomy in tastes and interests as well as a significant divergence in things of interest, generally speaking of course (I should know, being married for 28 years!). This rapport is often very effective in getting things going on a positive note, as it makes people immediately think that they share the same values and beliefs about something and might therefore have even more in common. I am not saying that this wouldn't happen with a feminine counterpart. I am simply saying that it is often more difficult as there is probably less commonality between the interests that I might share with a male counterpart – thus establishing rapport may take a bit more work!

Silver Bullet: Across the person-to-person communication interface, empathy is a key ability in understanding another person's perspective, motivation and behaviour.

4 Listening

The fourth and last rule is as important as all the others; perhaps more so, as I would suggest to you that it should be ubiquitous throughout the negotiation procedure – the ability to actively listen. The truth is that one of the key reasons why most of us are not effective communicators is simply because we're not very good at listening to other people. I remember being told once in the army that you have 'one mouth and two ears,' meaning that you should listen twice as much as you speak. I have never forgotten that. To listen effectively allows you to hear not only what is being said, but what is also not being said. Tone, volume and emphasis – these are all verbal clues as to what someone is saying. Sometimes an actual sentence or phrase in reality means the exact opposite. This is where we see the effects of sarcasm, hyperbole, litotes and so on manifest behind the actual words and give them possibly a different meaning. If you're not listening, you're going to miss this hidden dimension. It is imperative that when you are listening, you are focused and actively listening and not allowing your thoughts to drift off and distract you from your purpose at hand. Even a momentary lapse of a second or so might mean that you have missed something important. Now, some people are excruciating to listen to. I know, I've met many of them. Yet, we should pause and evaluate this. Speaking in a boring monotone is one of the greatest ways to 'switch off' those listening to you, couple it with waffle and unnecessary detail and you're on to a powerful distraction strategy. I assure you, the listening level will decrease exponentially the longer you prattle on and the irritation level will do the same in the opposite direction. Should you find yourself in the opposite situation (i.e. listening), one way to check if this is a deliberate distraction ploy or not is to focus completely on the party speaking. If you appear rapt in your attention, this may worry the other party that you have realised they are up to something. If you continue to give them your absolute undivided attention, you will begin to notice that the substance of what they are saying becomes more and more incoherent and disjointed. This is likely (assuming that they simply aren't a boring b★★★★★d) to manifest as they are – distracted in the first instance by being worried that their ploy has been discovered, and second, literally running out of things to say.

Silver Bullet: Take nothing for granted during a negotiation. Do not make assumptions based on what you see and hear. It is very easy to portray a particular character or stereotype to someone. Once they have identified you as such, it is very easy to manoeuvre safely from 'behind the mask.'

Listening has the added benefit of being a central plank in the scaffold of any future relationships. It can make you certain of the counterparty's actual position, and people appreciate it when they can see that you are interested in their views and opinions. This also shows courtesy and manners, which leaves a lasting good impression of your professionalism towards the matters at hand.

As mentioned at the start of this section, there are many ways in which people speak words and different people have different styles of communication. For the negotiator, this is very important as there are a number of connotations to this. The first of which is the idea of how the different styles of communication might negatively impact on one another, leading to the manifestation of conflict. I would group communication styles broadly into four main types:

1. Analytical/logical
2. Empathic
3. Relationship-orientated/driven
4. Detail-driven

Let's examine each of these styles, in turn, from an overview perspective. First, the analytical/logical communicator. These individuals are often from a scientific/engineering background. To them, what they want to say has to be broken down into the parts that create the whole. When they wish to transfer information (in my experience, this is how they view speaking), it must be presented in an ordered and logical manner. Often, they will also explain the background as to how they arrived at a particular conclusion or opinion so that you (the listener) will follow them through the (mental labyrinth?) twists and turns of reasoning and deduction, thus arriving at the same irrefutable conclusion. If you've ever listened to an analytical/logical communicator, it can often sound like the great reveal in some twisted murder plot staged in an isolated gothic manor during a ferocious storm. They are most closely aligned to the detail-driven communicator, but the fundamental difference is that they need to understand how the information (detail) links and connects towards some conclusion that is not always obvious to others. They want people to understand something *properly*. An example of this type of communicator:

> They will utilise a bigger negotiation team than us. This is because they will have different functional specialists present to address any specific questions – for example about engineering or finance related issues. I believe that this is also done as a show of strength and the belief that a bigger team will make us feel outnumbered and therefore at an inherent disadvantage. I think the key to maximising this to our benefit is twofold – either we ask lots of questions to divert away from the key/core issues, simultaneously gathering a lot of information that might be given inadvertently, or we don't ask many questions at all – giving the impression that we are comfortably informed concerning the matters at hand.

The key strength of the analytical communicator is thoroughness and supposition – taking known information and facts, analysing them and creating possible outcomes (i.e. anticipatory strategies). The key disadvantage to this kind of communicator is that they might be looking for an understanding that doesn't exist or spend time speculating on facts from a flawed perspective – arriving at erroneous conclusions.

The empathic communicator is probably on the opposite side of the communication continuum to the analytical/logical communicator. These individuals tend towards compromising and co-operation and really like to understand where the counterparties are coming from (i.e. why they have a particular stance, what is their motivation etc.). They will always seek a common solution and attempt to engineer a win/win scenario. They are very similar to the relationship-orientated/driven communicator, but the significant difference is that the relationship-driven communicator does not operate from an emotional perspective (i.e. the understanding mentioned above); rather, they attempt to construct a positive outcome for all parties by exploring the facts and options. An example of the empathic communicator:

> I think that this deal could be good for us. I feel that the environmental aspect is very important to them and that as we have

> a similar opinion and values on this subject, the joint venture makes sound sense as to a productive way forward. There is a positive synergy between the technological capabilities of our organisations and this translates well from a longer-term mutually beneficial perspective.

The main advantage of this type of communicator is that they might gain a deeper understanding of the other party's position (the why of behaviour and their position in the negotiation). The main disadvantage associated with this kind of communicator is that they are very emotive and may not make some decisions objectively.

The relationship-orientated/driven communicator, as mentioned above, is somewhat akin to an artist painting a picture or a weaver weaving a pattern. They are focused on achieving a positive outcome that benefits all parties to the process, but they do not operate from the emotive perspective. Rather, they will utilise facts as a catalyst for creating benefits, seeking to create synergies between the parties leading to the aforementioned win/win outcome.

An example of the relationship-orientated/driven communicator:

> Our existing infrastructure and geographically dispersed presence will facilitate a rapid deployment globally; allowing our partner companies to achieve a distribution previously out of their reach. In return, the revenue generated by the increased uptake of our resources by our partners will ensure our continued market leader position.

The main advantage of this kind of communicator is that they are often the glue in negotiating corporate joint ventures. What they say makes sense and the resultant synergies make sense from a business perspective for all concerned. The main disadvantage of this kind of communicator is that they may make excessive compromises, simply to arrive at some kind of deal without possibly considering the issues from a holistic perspective.

The detail-driven communicators – these kinds of individuals are often what many see as the hardcore negotiators who have all the facts at hand, understand the ramifications of them and is able to use them to leverage advantage during the process. Whilst it is absolutely 100% true that in commercial negotiations the devil really is in the detail and anyone involved should be as fully informed as they possibly can be, focus on detail alone is often detrimental to the less obvious, more subtle aspects of the negotiation ritual. This is the major disadvantage that this type of communicator literally brings to the table – an inability to see beyond the facts themselves. The major advantage of the detail-driven communicator, of course, is that of precision. If a counterparty makes a comment that is not accurate pertinent to the facts, then this is the individual who will home in on this and identify any discrepancy. Similarly, they are often the best placed to answer any questions from the counterparty due to their grip on the facts. This is a good person to have on the team and can be a powerful force for driving a positive outcome.

An example of the detail-driven communicator:

> The quantum of investment required for this project ($50 million), coupled with a long breakeven time horizon (15 years), makes this an unattractive prospect. I would suggest that our available financial resources are deployed on other identified investment opportunities contained in the documentation before you on the table.

Figure 3.1 shows where the different styles of communicator sit relative to one another.

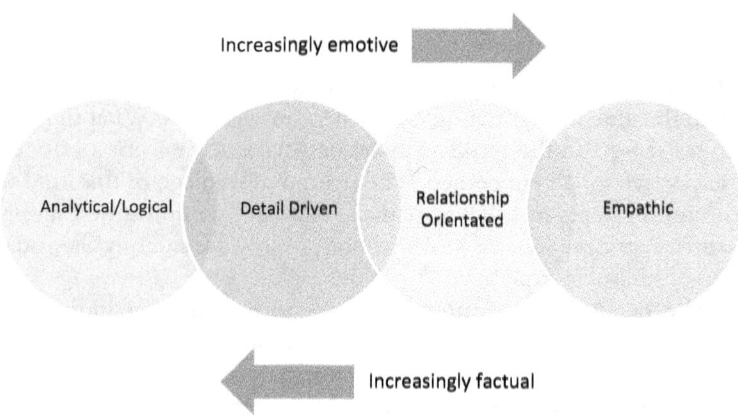

Figure 3.1 The Communication Continuum.

Silver Bullet: Mastering negotiation is achieved by mastering communication. The elite negotiator is able to draw from all of the different communication styles when needed to adapt to changing situations and dynamics within the negotiation ritual. They should be thought of as a communication chameleon – able to change with little effort as the situation or the strategy dictates.

Silver Bullet: In protracted, complex, multiparty negotiations, ensure that the individuals within the negotiation team comprise coverage of the different types of communicators.

Silver Bullet: All styles of communication within commercial negotiations are representative of either a subjective (emotive) approach or an objective (factual) approach. The extent of adoption of these approaches should be viewed as a continuum, as these approaches are often amalgamated in different quantities during the course of a negotiation by the individuals engaged within the process.

THE COMMUNICATION KEYS

There are a number of keys to understanding the underlying messages: meanings and purposes of what someone is saying and how they are saying it. For the negotiator, this is a very important skill to learn. I believe the first of these keys is the degree of animation that an individual is showing. Whilst there is a dark side to animation (i.e. anger, aggression, negative body language posture and gestures), I want to focus on the idea of whether or not someone is telling the truth. Normally (unless a person has been trained to an elite level), when something is close to us – perhaps a project that has been 'our baby' – we have a tendency to become quite animated when speaking about it. As we have been (or are) personally invested, this tends to reflect on our level of positivity. Individuals in this situation tend to have a very open body posture (not hiding something), their excitement is often palpable as is their enthusiasm. They will make a lot of hand gestures, many of which will be broad and encompassing (sweeping), they will make a lot of eye contact and will most often than not have a smiling or pleased expression on their face. Generally speaking, if such an individual is addressing you and behaving in this way, it is reasonably safe to assume that, at the very least, they believe what they are telling you is true (note the caveat of an elite trained negotiator, as this could be deliberate manipulation in their hands).

The second of the keys is to examine an individual who always appears to be playing the role of the 'Devil's Advocate' (from the counterparty – you know [hopefully!] what your team is doing). If someone is doing this frequently or excessively from across the table, this normally alerts my attention and I find myself focusing in on them and wondering just why it is that they seem unduly critical or difficult. In the author's experience, this is often an indicator that it is a **Deflection Strategy** (i.e. ensuring that the focus remains restricted). There may be a number of reasons for this. First, it's a great way to burn up time. Second, it keeps the control of the discussion with the counterparty. Third, and in conjunction with the preceding two points, it therefore keeps attention away from other things. Fourth, beware of the individual who uses expressions such as 'cards on the table,' or 'this is the unvarnished truth' or 'I'm telling you straight.' Quite often, expressions such as these mean the exact opposite! Consider when someone is telling you some outlandish story within a social setting prefaces the story with statements like 'I swear this is true' or 'I promise this is what happened' or 'you're not going to believe this.' In my experience, these sorts of statements are perfectly true (or true-ish) if they are coming from people who you know well and have worked/do work with closely. Within the social context, we all have a built-in assessor with friends that allows us to distinguish the extent of their exaggeration, making it possible to subtract the exaggeration – assuming, of course, the tall tale is not being told as a joke. If you find yourself within a negotiation scenario and you have someone at the table making statements like these, I would tread carefully and be quite cautious.

The fourth key is that of hyperbole or exaggeration, particularly of someone's position within a negotiation. So if the counterparties are constantly emphasising certain aspects or capabilities of themselves, they may well be trying to keep the attention away from those aspects within which they are weak or not wholly competent or do not want to come to light. Excessive hyping always makes me want to look for that which is not being said – to 'look beneath the surface and discover the true state of affairs.' It is fairly common for a human being to subconsciously adjust their verbal output and to skew it towards positive aspects rather than dwell on negative ones. Indeed, it is another form of deflection strategy, very similar to both the second and third keys discussed above.

Keys five and six should be considered as being constant and applicable to all the other keys – discovering things (facts and information) by focused observation and attentive listening (active listening).

The final key, number 7, should always serve as a word of caution – beware of (identify/assess/deal with) 'weaponised word strategies.' They are a very common form of verbal communication and, in my opinion, often a foolish tact to take. Nevertheless, they can be very effective, should a counterparty have the measure of your personality and perhaps know which buttons to press (or vice versa). Flattery, for instance, in the right circumstances can get you everywhere. We all like to be praised and everyone likes a compliment. Innuendo is a little more cunning to spot and one must be very careful not to become distracted, pondering what the other person was alluding or referring to.

Remember that I have largely been talking from the viewpoint of being on the receiving end (i.e. listening). Of course, there is a mirror image to all these keys and that is when (or if) you decide to utilise these strategies and techniques.

UNDERSTANDING NON-VERBAL COMMUNICATION

As mentioned earlier, it is generally accepted that the verbal aspects of communication are considered to be a small part of the overall communication process that takes place between people. The author thinks that the reason for this is probably an evolutionary factor. Whilst language is a powerful medium, at some point in our primitive past (prior to the development of verbal language), when there was a high degree of danger lurking around every corner either from other humans or a variety of large animals, the need to transmit, receive and understand a message with great rapidity was probably very important literally – your life could be on the line! A lot of how we process information, form opinions and decide courses of action are decided from a subconscious bias. We react to what we see in front of us – evolutionary hardwiring is at play – the knee-jerk almost autonomous reaction that has not been thought out. Whilst this is perfectly acceptable in quite a few circumstances (such as ducking to avoid something, not touching something) in order to keep us safe, I think that it is your enemy sitting alongside you at the negotiation table. It will cloud your mind and lead you down paths where you will arrive at flawed or erroneous conclusions. It will mislead you and deceive you!

I like to view the entire communication process as a vast mosaic composed of many different parts, all happening both simultaneously and sequentially. To see the picture, you have to encompass all the parts. This is absolutely true from a negotiation perspective. As mentioned above in the keys, one of the worst foibles most of us have is that we are unfocused listeners – we don't pay proper attention. Of course, to return to the mosaic analogy, let's consider some of the other pieces (factors) that will be at play that presents the picture that you see before you that influences your thoughts and responses.

A logical place to start in terms of what we see before us is that of physical appearance. There are two dimensions to this: what someone physically looks like and how they are dressed. First, let's consider looks. Everyone is different and from that perspective, everyone is unique, BUT society has groomed us all to an extent (particularly through the media and advertising) of what is considered handsome or beautiful or not, largely by the creation of stereotypes (discussed shortly) that portray an ideal. If you consider the conversation at the start of this section, there is also a lot of subconscious activity at work. Generally speaking, we are all drawn to nice looking people, and it would appear that on the whole, many good-looking people are more successful than not so good-looking counterparts if they are compared within the same environment and to the same criteria (all things being equal, of course). It has been postulated that physical looks also drive an evolutionary response – that better looks equates to better genetics, so this would be a better match for reproduction. The author has noticed on his travels around the world that there seems to be a general preponderance of better-looking people within those segments of the population that are wealthier. This aside, for whatever reason, it seems that those of us that are fortunate enough to be handsome/beautiful are generally treated with more attention than those of us who are not. Another aspect of appearance (which often complements looks) is that of physical build or figure. A fit individual (male or female) tends to be more confident than people who are perhaps unhappy or dissatisfied with some aspect(s) of themselves (most of us in reality, I suspect). Whilst this is all true, herein lies a warning: many are the beautiful butterflies who have flown too close to the flame, crashed and burned.

Do not make presumptions within a negotiation that you will be at an immediate advantage due to your genetic gifts. In some cases, depending on who the counterparties might be, this may be so, but for an elite negotiator, whilst they themselves might utilise any such advantage, they are unlikely to be swayed or influenced by it emanating from others. An interesting fact on this is that the author has noticed that men are more influenced by attractive women (in terms of being distracted, i.e. wanting to impress) than vice versa. Women negotiators tend to be more focused on the issues at hand and the process of reaching some result from the proceedings. I think that they (women) tend to be more pragmatic overall. In my experience, I have met some tough women around the negotiation table that knew how to drive a hard bargain.

Another aspect of appearance is, of course, how someone dresses. This is incredibly important as to how other people perceive you and it has many ramifications. I remember once being invited by a friend of mine, a recently retired senior army officer, to have breakfast with him and his wife in rather a nice restaurant in central London. As I was going to be attending a negotiation later that morning, I was suited and booted appropriately for the business that would shortly be at hand. I arrived a few minutes early and was shown to a table. Richard and his wife walked right past me (couldn't see me) and looked around the room. His eyes went right past me. Then I watched in amusement as they shot back to me and a look of surprise crossed his face. I had never met his wife before, and as introductions were made and they sat down opposite me, I could see that Richard was regarding me closely. I asked him what the matter was. He said simply that he'd never seen me dressed for business and cleanly shaven. He said I looked different. Then he said, 'You look powerful.' What I must share with the reader is that generally if I am working from home or at home (i.e. no face-to-face engagements), I tend to err very much on the scruffy side. My wife often laments the fact that in her opinion, I look like I've been sleeping rough in a park. A short while later, I had the pleasure of catching up with them at home and had reverted to my usual 'park chic.' Richard's wife found it very amusing from the opposite perspective, having only ever 'known me' dressed as a businessman. Need I say more? This is a perfect example of how dress influences appearance.

Perhaps one of the single most powerful aspects of non-verbal communication is that of the eyes. The old adage that the 'eyes are truly the window of the soul' always struck me. For starters, it is generally recognised that if someone refuses to look you in the eyes or looks away when speaking, they are lying or hiding something. Consider this: Have you ever met or been introduced to someone on a beach or other sunny setting and they are wearing mirrored sunglasses? If they don't take them off when they are introduced and keep wearing them during the conversation, then how does this make you feel? You are likely to have some kind of emotive response and it is not just because of the lack of manners on their part – you can't see their eyes, so you can't 'read' them properly, so you feel at a disadvantage. Quite often, you will see professional poker players wearing sunglasses at the table – I leave you to draw your own thoughts! What about the inverse? What emotive response would you feel if you had encountered someone pre-COVID with the lower half of their face masked? For the negotiator, it is of paramount importance to be able to read what is in other people's eyes whilst ensuring that you make eye contact every time you are speaking to someone. In a group setting, ensure that you 'travel' the room, making eye contact with different individuals as you speak, as this generally denotes truthfulness and belief in what you are saying. A key thing to watch out for is rapid blinking, as this tends to denote uncertainty at best or possibly deceit. Note what is said about this in the following paragraph.

A wider dimension to the issues discussed above is that of facial expression. Often, our facial expression can give lie to the words coming from our mouths. How many times have you encountered someone who is clearly angry or upset (by their facial expression) who denies that they are? I would suggest that facial expression is a major element within the dimension of the non-verbal aspects of negotiation. A good way to get a quick grasp on this is to consider an individual's facial expression as they walk past you on the street. Let's imagine that they look bad-tempered or grumpy. You think to yourself 'bad-tempered so and so,' then you see them meet some friends and they smile and look like a completely different person. As mentioned earlier, be careful of making snap judgements about what you see before you. A seeming bad-tempered individual sitting across the table from you might just turn out to be your greatest ally! During a negotiation, you must be aware of the fact that your face can reveal your inner thoughts; so a 'poker face' – making your expression enigmatic or unreadable can be an advantage. The elite trained negotiators know how to use their facial expression (or lack thereof) as a powerful tool; being able to 'play their face' to influence the perceptions of counterparties, as in a negotiation, the face is watched intently by everyone (or should be!). Some of the key aspects to watch: if someone is looking up at you whilst their head is downcast is often a sign of evaluation of you and what you are saying. Frowning can indicate confusion, irritation or annoyance, whilst a clenched jaw and trembling lips are strong indicators of anger. However, trembling lips when coupled with rapid blinking can be an indication of emotional upset or sadness.

It is also important to understand that the non-verbal behaviour of an individual is always likely to be influenced by two aspects of culture, both of which are relevant to the corporate setting. First, their national culture. In the author's view, where someone comes from, has grown up, lays the foundational imprint of their behavioural norms, values and beliefs. This does tend to become diluted by both time and space (i.e. residing in another country for a long period), subconsciously adopting behavioural traits of social circle/work colleagues and so forth, but the essence remains. There is a huge variation in accepted cultural behaviours and values, and it is the duty of the negotiator to be fully conversant with each and every one, particularly within the domain of international/multinational negotiations. The negotiation graveyard is littered with the bodies of those who failed to understand what might or might not sink a deal due to cultural factors and the ever-present scope for misunderstandings. The second aspect of culture that will influence the behaviour of counterparties is that of their organisational culture. Every organisation is different and it too has an accepted set of values, beliefs and normative behaviours that employees are expected to conform and subscribe to, at least during working hours. I have found that sometimes the organisational way is actually a significant block to a successful outcome or, at best, leads to protracted processes that do no one any favours. Once again, I would suggest to the reader that this should form part of your preparation: that you have an awareness of how a particular organisation thinks and what non-verbal information this might convey.

Another aspect of non-verbal behaviour (and interestingly, very much allied to culture) is that of the use of hand gestures. Wide sweeping gestures tend to denote exuberance and excitement. Some hand gestures, when accompanied by a nodding head, serve to act as re-enforcers of what is being said. If someone covers or partially obscures their mouth when talking, this is generally believed to be a sign of dishonesty, whilst hands in pockets indicate insecurity. If someone is rubbing the back of their head whilst looking around the room, this is often considered to be a sign of building frustration. If someone is resting their head on their hands, this might denote a loss of focus/interest in proceedings. People who stand with their hands on their hips in a wide stance are often taken to be confident and comfortable, whilst excessive, uncoordinated gestures may denote unease or tension.

Closely allied to the factors discussed in the preceding paragraphs, this is further compounded by proxemics. In my experience, I have found that different cultures have different proximity ranges, that is, how close they stand to one another when interacting. Some examples that spring immediately to mind: African nations tend to be in close proximity when talking, whilst the British hold a wider distance. Latin Americans, however, interact within a very close proximal distance accompanied with a high degree of touching, as do Arabic people. The accepted proximal distance tends to be directly reflective of culture.

Silver Bullet: Proxemics is often a neglected area when preparing for a negotiation across cultures.

Coupled closely with proxemics, it is important to have an understanding of what is called haptic (touch). Among the many dimensions of non-verbal communication, I would suggest to the reader that touch is very powerful. First, it is very contextual – so how a mother strokes the cheek of her baby and the information that conveys is far different from someone getting slapped in the face for being rude. Even from this simple example, it becomes evident that the role of touch carries significant meaning. Touch in all its forms is very emotive and as such has the capacity to reflect the entire ambit of human emotions. Touch tends to be an amplifier of the spoken word and, I believe, the most significant method of communication when it comes to building relationships and trust with others.

The author believes that there are 'three deadly sins' within the realm of non-verbal communication: preconceptions, subconscious association and stereotypes. Having preconceived ideas is obviously a dangerous tack to take, as they might be based on your own perception, incorrect information and facts or simply bias. Subconscious association is when our brains decide something by making assumptions from our knowledge base. This is extremely detrimental to understanding a situation as it really might be not what it appears to be. For example, if you are driving down the road and you see someone standing at a zebra crossing, your brain assumes that they are there because they are about to cross the road. Without sounding like a spy movie, are they though? A man wearing a uniform and driving a delivery van is obviously delivering parcels. Someone sitting on a pier or harbour wall with a fishing rod in their hands is there because they are fishing and someone sitting opposite you in a suit who introduces themselves as 'Head of Legal' must be so – right? I leave the reader to ponder this. Stereotyping is another example of our brain taking short cuts, utilising if/then paradigms – what we see before us is what must be the obvious truth – right?

Silver Bullet: In the realm of non-verbal communication, there are three deadly sins – preconceptions, subconscious association and stereotypes.

In light of the point made about stereotyping above, I would like to introduce you to my friend Smithy. I often do this in my negotiation classes, as it serves to prove this point very concisely. You, the reader, will unfortunately have to rely on your own mental visualisation, but the important thing will be to be honest with yourself. So, Smithy is six feet and six inches tall, fairly muscley, has tattoos on both forearms, a shaven head and a serious look on his face. So the question is: What do you think he does for a living? There is always a range of answers, but most of them seem to revolve around being a bodyguard or a bouncer and so on.

Well, you probably thought something similar yourself. Smithy, however, is a very senior manager in the international oil and gas industry, is a Chartered Engineer and has an MBA and an engineering undergraduate degree. He is soft spoken, has a good sense of humour and is a popular guy. I rest my case.

In conclusion, consider the scenario below. I leave it to the reader to ponder this for themselves, but believe that it is a good exercise of consideration of this chapter's topic.

Scenario: On the day that you and a colleague go to close and sign a significant contract, you notice the following things:

> The receptionist who is always smiley and slightly flirtatious looks up at you both warily when you enter the office. Avoiding eye contact, she queries why you're there, which is surprising to you. She hesitantly picks up the phone, turning around in her chair with her back to you, head bent hunched to the mouthpiece. You are unable to hear what she is saying. She finishes the call and turns back to face you. She asks if you would like some coffee and you notice that she is keeping her distance from you both and also waving her hands around. As she goes to make coffee, you notice that she is washing her hands with invisible soap. Presently, the door opens and someone whom you are not quite sure as to who they are steps forward, extending a hand. His grip is firm and he is staring you straight in the eyes. He informs you that his colleagues with whom you had negotiated the contract to be signed are not available. You are led into an unfamiliar room, sparsely furnished and poorly lighted. It appears to you as if this is some sort of spare, disused room. As you sit down, you notice that this individual glances at his watch. You notice his forehead crease with a momentary frown. He looks up at you both and purses his lips. He exhales noisily and begins to speak … up to this moment what are your thoughts?

4

MANAGING STRESS AND CONTROLLING CONFLICT

Negotiation is a stressful business. The process is often, despite the most careful preparation, indeterminate, as the outcome lies shrouded in the opaque mists of the future. Random events can manifest, altering the course of the negotiation in an instant. Whether you are acting solo or part of a team, you must remember that stress can manifest at any given moment. Stress is dangerous. It can disrupt performance and destroy any positive outcome. Stress walks hand in hand with conflict and is often the progenitor to it. Some stress is good and this stress should be harnessed. 'Good' stress is something that motivates, makes you want to rise to the challenge, makes you want to win, to perform, whilst 'bad' stress challenges your belief in yourself, makes you feel hopeless, drains your energy and saps your desire to achieve. It undermines your confidence and demotivates.

The strange thing about stress though is that it is personal. We are all unique and as a consequence of this, different things affect us in different ways. For instance, I have happily had tarantula's sitting on my face when I was in Africa – I had collected them myself from their burrows out in the bush – I have always found all wildlife fascinating. Contrast this to a guy I knew in Scotland; if there was a nature documentary on the television and it was about spiders, he would start vomiting from across the room. In both the personal and corporate sense, stress is bad news indeed, from a performance perspective (corporate) and from a health perspective (personal). The onset of stress (bad stress) is when you perceive that you have an inability to cope – it's all quite literally in your mind! This perception is brought about by something that triggers this thought process and you feel you can no longer cope. Figure 4.1, the Stress Causation

DOI: 10.4324/9781003263722-4

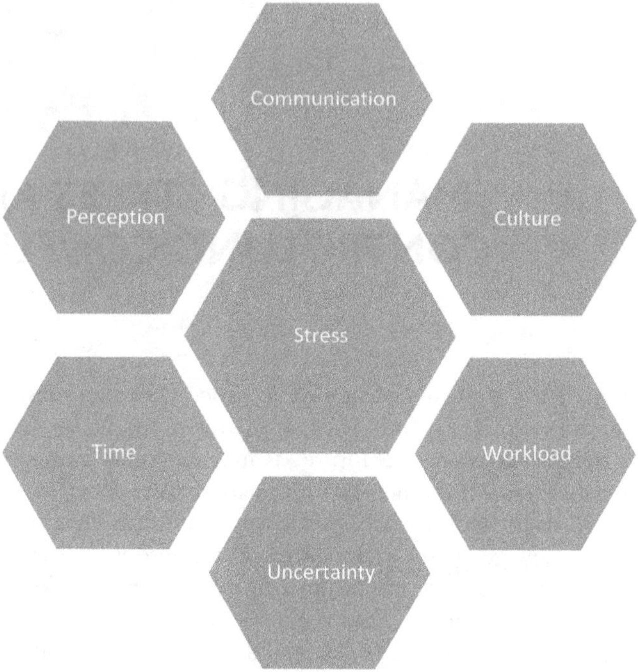

Figure 4.1 The Stress Causation Paradigm.

Paradigm, is exceptionally useful in identifying and analysing the different contributing factors. I have used it many times to nullify and mitigate stress before it becomes a functional problem. This model is good if you are operating solo and is also very useful when you are part of a negotiation team.

THE STRESS CAUSATION PARADIGM

As can be seen from Figure 4.1, I believe that there are six factors that contribute to the onset of stress. When utilising this model for an analysis, it is important to understand that each factor should be examined and considered on a case-by-case basis as not all of them will carry an equal contribution towards the prevalent stress level. They will differ between individuals and situations. For the sake of a structured approach here (and for no other reason), let's examine these different factors clockwise.

1 Communication

From the perspective of utilising this model, the communication dynamic should be assessed in terms of quality of communication. For the solo negotiator, you should consider how effective you believe the dialogue to have been thus far. Simple, honest appraisal is what is needed here. Have you been clear in statements that you have made? Does the counterparty understand your position? Have you said or omitted to say something that could have moved the process forward, but perhaps should've been phrased with more clarity or withheld more discreetly? Do you understand the counterparty's position? Have they said something that is unclear and as yet, you have not sought clarification? What is the level of ambiguity present? Poor communication, coupled with the ever-present scope for misunderstandings, will feed directly into the level of stress being felt by participants in the process. Think before you speak. Consider your statements. Question anything that you don't understand completely. If you feel something has been misrepresented or misconstrued around the table, then bring it up and address it.

2 Culture

The key to ensuring that this does not become a problem and amplify the situation stressfully is to be prepared. In an earlier discussion, we examined the 'twin cultures' that impact and influence everyone within the corporate setting: a person's national culture and their organisational culture. Considering the national cultural aspects first, this is where things can go swiftly awry, particularly within a cross-cultural setting. If this does happen (perhaps due to an unintended slight or insult), then the stress level is going to ratchet up rapidly. One of the best ways of ensuring that you and/or your team don't find yourself in this position is to refrain from any conversation relating to religion and politics – and it is never a good idea to test out a different cultures' sense of humour by telling them a joke (I have seen this cause spectacular damage), nor to comment (even if asked to do so) about a particular country's policy or what is happening there at present. From the organisational cultural perspective, being prepared and familiar with the company in question and having a thorough understanding of how it does business ensures that your approach is tailored in the right manner to complement rather than antagonise (i.e. keeping things on a positive footing around the negotiation table). It is important to understand that even away from the table, the wrong thing said, or opinion expressed over a cup of coffee or at the lunch table can have dire consequences.

3 Workload

Perhaps the most ubiquitous dimension of causing stress in the workplace today is that of workload. Organisations seem bent on streamlining departments in order to become more cost-effective. What this translates into, for example, is that there used to be six people in a department – it's cut to four – yet the four remaining individuals are expected to shoulder the workload for six! I think of this as corporate insanity, and to me, it has never made sense. For the negotiator(s) about to become embroiled within a complex, lengthy process, this problem can be ameliorated by ensuring that the background work is done comfortably ahead of time and that, if in a team scenario, no one has a disproportionate burden. This sometimes simply occurs and using this model to probe and inspect this factor is a sensible and valuable thing to do to ensure that stress is mitigated if not nullified completely (relative to this factor).

4 Uncertainty

When a human being is not sure of something, they find it (to some degree) stressful. This is because we like to know what we are doing it and why. This is fundamental psychological behaviour. Unfortunately, as the outcome of a negotiation is not certain by any means, then it is certain to be a stressor element. One way to reduce or mitigate this problem is to attempt to foresee likely outcomes. In the author's experience, the best way to achieve this is through the generation of scenarios. It is always good to construct three scenarios: a worst case (pessimistic), a best case (optimistic) and a likely case (realistic). There is no guarantee that you will be on the mark, as ultimately, we can't know the future. Consider this: if the outcome was known or at least almost predictable, then there would be little, if any, need for negotiation and negotiators. I will talk about this later when discussing the due diligence process. Suffice to say, the better your information and the better informed you are, the better decisions you are likely to make. This model is useful within the team dynamic, as it can serve as a checkpoint that the team members are all on the same page. Sometimes the uncertainty of an individual might be through a misunderstanding or not having heard/read some particular information. This might be easily correctable if someone else is able to remove this by simply informing them (assuming the relevant information is known to other team members).

5 Time

I think that time is the major cause of stress within negotiations. All too often, an agreement must be made or a deal struck with the clock ticking towards some predetermined deadline. There is a duality to time and, I guess, it depends on your position within the negotiation. If you are the more powerful party and do not have the same time constraints as the counterparty, then it is a common tactic to 'drag your feet' if it serves your purpose in putting the other side under increased pressure to achieve a result. The best way to mitigate this stressor is to be prepared, have a good plan (that has inherent flexibility within it to adapt as required) and to manage time itself to ensure that milestones in the agenda are reached when they need to be. To achieve this, you will need to establish a modicum of control over the proceedings, but this should be factored into your plan and how your strategy for the negotiation is executed. No matter what you do though, never waste time.

Silver Bullet: Time that is lost is lost forever – you cannot make up for it, nor reclaim it in some manner. Give time concentrated attention prior, during and post negotiation. Mismanagement of time is often a valuable lesson to learn.

6 Perception

I often state to delegates on my negotiation courses that 'there is no such thing as reality, only perception.' Stop and think about this for a moment; it is not quite as radical and 'out there' as it may first seem. The truth is that if we were able to look through each other's eyes and see how we all understand the same situation or environment in so many different ways and permutations, we'd probably be very surprised. For the negotiator, the author would suggest that this is another dimension to empathy. I like to call it the **psycho-empathic overlay** and it is a technique that I have honed over the years to a fine art (I believe!).

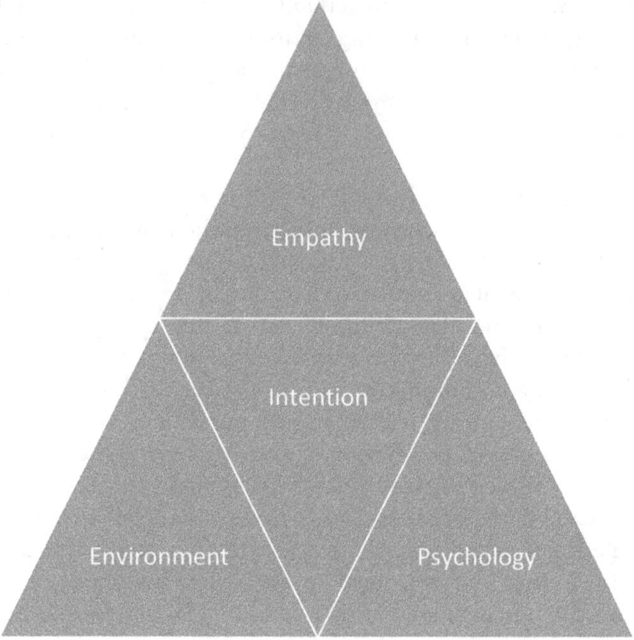

Figure 4.2 The Psycho-empathic Overlay Model.

Information comes from a variety of sources. The environment provides us with information – lighting, seating arrangements, access to IT, refreshment/toilet facilities, location of negotiation venue (home ground, neutral, counterparty ground) – as do people by both their words and actions (see previous section on verbal/non-verbal communication). How you recognise and assimilate this information is the key to being successful. The reader will notice in Figure 4.2 that intention is the central aspect. Negotiation is about choice and choice is informed by intention. This model represents that your degree of empathy with the counterparty will shape your intention, but that this intention will be tempered by a clear evaluation and assessment of both the environment within which you find yourself and the psychological factors that you either knew beforehand about the counterparty or are witnessing around the table 'live.' Clarity in your own mind as to your intentions (either immediate/short and/ or longer term) will guide and shape your behaviour during the process. The author has always found that focus this way allows adaptability as the situation unfolds. Your empathy level can change as behaviour and environmental factors may alter (perhaps the behaviour of the counterparty swings from co-operative to aggressive). This model will also give you the ability to mask your true intention if needed (poker face), a skill that cannot be overstated in terms of importance to the commercial negotiator, especially when you are trying to shape the perceptions of others.

As established thus far, stress is dangerous and unique to the individual. When operating as part of a negotiation team (consider the Stress Causation Paradigm), it is imperative that stress doesn't spread. I have always believed that stress is infectious – it can transmit from one person to another very rapidly – even though the stress that is spread by one individual may well be different in the infected individual (i.e. stressed for a different reason; e.g. the failure of someone to finish something places an increased workload onto someone else or puts them under time pressure due to the delay). Operating solo, this is easier to contain, as you only have yourself to get under control from a stress perspective. In a team-based scenario, it is imperative that you (assuming you're the team leader) pay close attention to the monitoring and subsequent control of stress beginning to manifest.

A procedure for managing stress:

1 Be in control

- Focus on having a positive attitude towards the proceedings
- Be adaptable – have awareness of likely scenarios and always generate/consider options
- Plan and manage time

2 Be calm

- Identify and analyse potential stressors
- Avoid making assumptions
- Centre yourself – do not let the behaviour or words of others unbalance you

3 Be rationale

- Make value judgements
- Consider the longer-term relationship possibilities

DECISION FATIGUE

Negotiations, just like people, are all different. Should you find yourself involved within a high pressure, high stake negotiation, particularly if it is prolonged or a complex, protracted process, then the author would suggest that you pay particular attention to the concept of decision fatigue. Decision fatigue is exactly what it says on the tin: a mental tiredness that will negatively impinge upon your ability to make decisions. During a protracted negotiation, there will always be points that represent real dangers. I call these 'Decision Fatigue Zones' (DFZ). In a DFZ, your concentration is lapsing, you are mentally tired (or exhausted) and physical discomfort begins to manifest. When you are within this zone, you may begin to feel overwhelmed with the number of decisions facing you and you will reach a place of decision-making overload. This is a mental saturation point and it will most certainly impede any clarity in further decision-making.

Silver Bullet: Decision fatigue and decision fatigue zones are a major stressor within the negotiation process. They are very dangerous as they impede the ability to make clear decisions. These must be avoided at all costs (if you are subject to them, unless you are using them as a tactic on the counterparty). Call a break: halt proceedings, regroup and recharge.

The Silver Bullet above mentions the fact that driving a negotiation process to the point of decision fatigue setting in could be (and is) a very effective tactic to utilise on the counterparty. I have always thought of this not unlike a saturation diver, a 'time in process' metric where there is an optimal amount of time to be spent engaged within a particular activity, after which it is possibly detrimental. The author mentioned time earlier and stated that insufficiency of time was often a primary driver for the manifestation of stress. Time pressure in terms of achieving a wide scope around the negotiation table (i.e. this is the only window available), when utilised deliberately to ensure that the counterparty will arrive at a decision fatigue zone, is a very powerful negotiation strategy.

A notable example of this is when I was present in a particular country and a delegation representing a joint venture (JV) group (who wanted to expand the JV with this particular country's NOC

(National Oil Company) arrived for 'high-level conclusive talks' (you've got to love corporate parlance!). An interesting dimension to this story is that I think that the major cause of difficulty here was a cultural difference regarding work ethics and time management; however, I stand behind statements made thus far about preparation pre-negotiation throughout this book: the visiting team should've been prepared. Another aspect sub-contextual here was that the NOC had the power, not the visiting party. The NOC used this power very craftily, by setting the meeting for a Friday morning. I was invited to watch the proceedings as a guest. I had no involvement, advisory or otherwise. As this is what I do, I accepted the invitation and sat back to watch and listen with great interest. A series of interminable presentations ensued, with breaks for coffee and lunch. The day wore on; I could see that individuals were starting to approach the 'decision fatigue zone' – becoming fidgety and loosing concentration (clearly evidenced with body language such as checking watches, phones, and looking around the room). The NOC did not call any afternoon breaks. I watched the DF firm its hold upon the visitors (another dimension to always pay attention to is location; the visitors had already had a flight and a lengthy airport transfer journey – deliberately, I believe, to ensure that they were that little bit more tired prior to the start of proceedings). A number of preliminary, peripheral matters were concluded and agreed upon, yet the core or heart of the matter had yet to be directly touched upon (I believe the NOC team were following a deliberate strategy on this, as unbeknownst to the visitors, there were other parties making representations for the same deal the following week – so were happy to trundle along and take things slow, keeping all their options open). It got to 4pm. The most senior man from the NOC stood and stopped the current talks then and there and announced that it was time to go home. I remember vividly the shock on the visitors' faces, the disbelief and a bit of irritation turning to anger. The most senior member of the visiting delegation wanted to know, in no uncertain terms, just what the hell was going on. He was regarded coolly (remember points on poker face?) and informed that it was now the start of the weekend and that if the visitors couldn't be efficient with their time, then perhaps they should rebook another appointment at a later date to resume discussions. The NOC party left the room and went home. The visiting team of negotiators failed to close the deal in due course, and I believe that they were outclassed in terms of who they were negotiating with. I think they were manipulated every step of the way, even in so far as when these parties did meet again a week or so later, there was some animosity on the part of those who'd felt they'd wasted their time on the first visit and were now a bit impatient and more aggressive to close the deal. They had been placed under a higher level of stress without even realising it and I have no doubt that this compromised their efficiency. The NOC negotiation team remained unperturbed, completely calm and fully in control. The author would suggest to the reader that a consideration of many of the sub-elements of this short tale would not go amiss as a clear and precise example of negotiation strategies and tactics that can be employed.

The second element of this chapter is that on managing conflict. As mentioned, I believe that stress is often the progenitor of conflict and is far more easily controlled if caught early. The author calls this The Fire Principle, as just like a fire, they all start small, but if ignored, they can quickly escalate into something that is out of control. Conflict is the nemesis of productive negotiation and unless being deliberately engineered (yes, it can be a strategy and/or a tactic), should be avoided and prevented at all costs as it can cause irreconcilable damage to a potential longer-term relationship. Often, if we consider how and where conflict of any form originated, we would probably realise (with the remarkable clarity bestowed by hindsight) that it was unnecessary and probably could've been avoided or stopped with relatively little effort. Keeping to the fire analogy, I believe that the extinguishers of conflict are the following:

1 Awareness

A central thread or vein that runs throughout this book is the concept of being prepared. Whilst this suggests that this is pre-emptive and put into place prior to a negotiation starting, I would like to suggest that preparation entails an ongoing commitment of awareness. The negotiator must 'be aware' of the subtle nuances occurring around the table – they must be able to 'see' when something needs redress or a slight course correction to prevent the entire process from floundering until founding upon the jagged rocks of failure. I believe that in most cases, conflict can be removed if you are aware of it beginning to manifest and are able to take appropriate action.

2 Communication

Although seemingly obvious and already covered thus far, the best way to ameliorate or mitigate conflict is to talk, draw it out into the open; often, the conflict may well be as a result of a miscommunication or a misunderstanding and this can be cleared up generally quickly and without undue effort, restoring the process back onto a productive path forward. The author has found that when conflict is at an evolutionary stage, someone could have highlighted the issue, yet felt uncomfortable (or awkward/embarrassed) to bring it up possibly due to the fear of causing discomfort or loss of face to the counterparty or any other individual present. Should you find yourself in this position, the author suggests that you call a break and perhaps address the matter informally with a quiet word with your opposite number, perhaps over a cup of tea or coffee; this has been an approach of mine throughout my time around the negotiation table.

3 Empathy

Sometimes the behaviour of an individual is caused by some underlying factor that is not known or immediately evident. Although I have discussed empathy already and its importance within the communication paradigm, sometimes being able to 'lift the veil' by considering a situation from the perspective of the counterparty can lead you to a place of understanding which will enable you to diffuse any conflict that has arisen or is beginning to manifest. Observe and listen. Quite often the clues are there.

Silver Bullet: Conflict is very similar to fire. They all start small, but if left unattended, may quickly grow out of control.

The costs of conflict in negotiations:

- Wasted time
- Loss of focus
- Emotive/subjective factors
- Financial implications
- Loss of trust

- Implications for future business relationships
- Direct costs of Alternative Dispute Resolution (ADR)/ litigation

Conflict resolution:
Five key steps:

1 Identify core causal factors/items

- Is there a fundamental incompatibility with each side's position?
- Is it a clash of styles/cultures?

2 Engage in root cause analysis (RCA)

- What was the conflict initiator?
- Did you make unrealistic assumptions pre-negotiation?
- Did you fundamentally misunderstand the other party's expectations?
- Are there stakeholders who were not identified?

3 Encourage open, honest dialogue

- Shows willingness to move towards resolution
- Provides opportunity to review both parties' positions

4 Be willing to compromise

- Do not consider the negotiation to be a zero-sum game
- Review your alternatives and options
- Identify what you can trade that is not important to you but is to the other side; shows compromise (burn off)

5 Utilise empathy

- Explore to discover underlying reason for other party's position or behaviour

EMOTIONAL EQUILIBRIUM

I believe that this is perhaps the most important skill and trait for the modern negotiator to possess. Emotional equilibrium to me represents mental stillness, calmness, a zen-like state where all decisions and judgements are made in a reasoned fashion after careful contemplation and consideration. There is no stress, there is no conflict in your mind. You possess great clarity in what you are doing and why. Importantly, when you can achieve emotional equilibrium, decision-making becomes enhanced as you mentally control uncertainty: not engaging in pointless, repetitive and time wasting 'what if' mental games with yourself. In this state, you possess a certainty, a serenity that imparts an impassiveness that gives nothing away and allows you to control your reactions should new facts suddenly be brought to light. True emotional equilibrium is the domain of the elite level practitioner – one who truly understands negotiation and all of its complexities. It is a worthy aspiration to want to master this and join the ranks of the elite practitioners.

In order to achieve the state of emotional equilibrium around the negotiation table, there are a number of elements that you need to address. It is an old adage that 'everything is down to attitude.' Personally, I subscribe to this. There are only two types of attitudes (discounting neutral) with which to approach anything: a positive attitude or a negative one. Consider this: many things are outwith our control, a negative stance does nothing. It does not improve the situation, but it may change it for the worse in the longer term. A negative attitude prevents the materialisation of positivity. Therefore, it can spread and effect a wider spectrum of happenings and circumstances. In fact, it may prevent anything good arising from something that has occurred detrimentally (i.e. losing a contract on narrow grounds and not bothering to renegotiate the next time an opportunity may arise with the same counterparty). A negative attitude destroys confidence and self-belief. It fosters apathy for learning what went wrong and how to prevent it occurring again. It implies that the game is lost and there is no point in trying any more. However, a positive attitude has the capability of nullifying and reversing all these aspects. True; if you've lost a contract, you won't magically get it back, but you may review what happened and learn a valuable lesson. I believe that positivity is infectious and people are drawn to working with you. A positive attitude also places you ready to grasp emergent opportunities, it will allow you to 'roll with the punches' and expect the unexpected – show no reaction and be fluid in your strategy and the tactics that you will employ.

One of the most powerful things that I have ever learned to do is what I like to call Mental Benchmarking. This is one of my secrets that I feel is right to share with you, my readers, who have after all supported me by purchasing a copy of this book! All of us are the sum product of our experiences; this is something that we cannot get away from, nor change (though we all continuously change as we gain experience and learn more). Mental Benchmarking is very simple in essence. All it requires is for you to consider the current situation within which you may find yourself. This might not be comfortable or even far from ideal, but consider it carefully and without emotion, do not cloud your thinking process, don't let your thoughts run away with you – control your imagination. Next, search back through your life's memories and identify the worst situation that you have ever found yourself in – the point at which you were at your lowest ebb. The realisation will dawn on you that you are standing here at some future point; that you got through that terrible time; you survived, moved on and encountered many wondrous and happy things. What you must then do is compare your current situation/problem with this blackest or most difficult memory and it is very likely that you will realise that this situation (I sincerely hope) pales by comparison. This will allow you to draw from that time and experience and will translate into a recognition that you have some control in this process and that it's not going to beat you. It will impart objectivity and allow you to focus on what needs to be done, keeping you on track. Whenever the chips have been down, this is exactly what I do, and I have always found it to be a great source of inspiration in overcoming difficult situations.

5

STYLES OF NEGOTIATORS

Negotiations, like people, are unique and the different people who participate in negotiations will have different styles as to how they operate. In my opinion, there are only three overarching stylistic approaches: they can be competitive, co-operative or a combination thereof (different parts of the same negotiation may switch through these three options depending on what transpires around the table or what a particular party's strategy might be). It is important to understand that no matter how a counterparty might present themselves to you, there will always be some underpinning rationale as to why they have adopted a particular style and attitude when seated across the table; as mentioned previously, it may even be a ploy to conceal their real intentions. However, if you can understand why the counterparty is evidencing a particular approach or set of behavioural traits, then you have a powerful invisible ally at your side. For example, it may be possible to take action to alter the counterparty's strategy, perhaps by addressing some underlying issue that hasn't come out into the open, thus recalibrating the negotiation's current status. Additionally, if you realise that the behaviour is just a ploy, you can utilise this by going along with it leading the counterparty to believe that you have been fooled. This gives you a barrier from which to work behind in the furtherance of your own agenda.

No matter the situation or (to a lesser degree) any intentions of the parties, there are two factors that underpin everything that happens at the negotiation table. First, there's the power dimension. There is often (if not nearly always) an imbalance within a commercial negotiation between the parties. Power is dictated by a range of factors, which will be discussed later. Needless to say, those with the

DOI: 10.4324/9781003263722-5

power tend to use it to their advantage. Second, as mentioned already, is the problem of self-interest. When coupled together, power might well be abused in the furtherance of self-interest. The reader may recall that self-interest might be personal (i.e. what's in it for me?), or might be representative of an organisational perspective (what's in it for us – the organisation?) or even a combination of both. I highlight these two factors as in my opinion they are often the two major road blocks to a mutually successful outcome.

In addition to the two cardinal points above, there is a range of other important factors that should be considered when trying to understand the style adopted by a negotiator. The obvious place to start is the personality of those who may be sitting across the table from you; again, the reader should hear echoes of 'being prepared' in their mind, so you try to find out as much as you can about the individual(s) in question as part of your due diligence procedures: how they generally behave, what do they react to, what are their beliefs and opinions about things. This helps if the counterparties in question have negotiated with you before or if they are known to other colleagues within your organisation. A further factor must consider the nature of what is being negotiated. Is it sensitive? Is it important? Are there social connotations connected to/associated with the outcome? Is it high profile and being watched by the media? Could it damage our corporate reputation? Do we have a stakeholder engagement plan? A media liaison plan? Are we able to control the external factors associated with the outcome of this negotiation?

Once the negotiation is 'live,' you must observe, listen and evaluate the behaviour of the counterparty. You should question why they are behaving in a particular manner (see earlier paragraph) and assess the potential reasons why. A big central issue that might answer many of the facets of this conversation is whether or not the negotiation is a one-off or there is a longer-term intention of the parties to establish an ongoing, longer-term relationship. If I am not being indelicate, consider as a parallel the difference between a holiday romance for a few days and meeting the person whom you are going to marry – there are significant differences, factors at play and decisions to be made between the two. The final issue that I would like to mention here is to consider how clear and defined you are in terms of your goals and objectives, how you intend to achieve them (your strategy and tactics) and how the pursuit of these is going to dictate your chosen style. The author cannot understate how important it is to spend time on these issues as a grasp of them often equals significant success.

When considering the stylistic approach to a negotiation (from both the counterparty and your perspective), it is important to recognise that there are no dictates set in stone, no universal prescription of 'this is how negotiate.' As the author has stated previously, every negotiation is a unique set of circumstances, factors, individuals and occurrences – flexibility and adaptability must be your key watchwords.

Silver Bullet: There are two cardinal points that predominantly impact upon and shape the course of a commercial negotiation –the relative balance of power between the parties and their self-interest.

Silver Bullet: No universal prescription exists as to 'how to' conduct a negotiation. The ability to adapt and be flexible is of paramount importance.

THE COMPETITIVE STYLE OF NEGOTIATION

This is a harder approach to negotiation. The overriding perspective here is often the fulfilment as much as possible of self-interest with little regard to the position or interest of the counterparty. Often it is a pressure approach. This may be in the form of time limitations, a bombardment of technical and financial information, introducing new issues suddenly – generally trying to magnify the counterparty's disadvantages whilst maximising their own – it is a style that is designed to deliberately keep the counterparty off balance. If you adopt a pure form of this style, be aware of the obvious ramifications that it will often create a win/lose situation (depending, of course, on whether or not you particularly care or are successful) and this is only likely to present negative connotations for any longer-term involvement or commitment.

The common behavioural features that tend to be exhibited when this style is adopted is generally aggression and attempting to intimidate (see points above) through bullying, being intractable and inflexible regarding position and the imposition of deadlines ('take it or leave it' syndrome). The competitive negotiator seeks to maximise their advantage at all times. Another common aspect of this style is to be oblique, to be deliberately vague or misleading, to be unhelpful and feign ignorance, to be evasive in answering questions or clarifying facts. The intention is to manipulate the other party to their disadvantage. The reader must remember that this could all be an act and that the other party could be bluffing. The author once knew a CEO of a fairly large company who was notoriously rude and aggressive in his dealings with everyone (as far as I know, I can think of no exceptions). He leveraged his power to the max (his company was the single source supplier of a very sought-after proprietary technology). He dictated, he spoke, he didn't listen nor was he interested in the opinions of others. He was completely disinterested in relationships with other parties. His only interest was maximising his revenue and profit. He was universally disliked – but he didn't care! He ruled his organisation through fear and frequently dismissed employees for the smallest transgressions. If anyone ever threatened legal action, he would encourage them to 'go for it' as he would 'relish breaking them in a court.' These people are out there and they may not be pretending.

Such extreme examples aside, the competitive style of negotiation is normally carefully planned out and a defined agenda is closely followed even if this may not appear to be the case (often that's the very point). The intention is to leave the negotiation table with the biggest possible share of the spoils, whatever they might be. It is always necessary when faced with this style of negotiator (as opposed to utilising it) to attempt to look behind the language and behaviour – attempt to assess to what degree the counterparty might be masking – that is, trying to present a picture to you that they want you to believe and accept at face value.

The competitive style should be considered as a linear process. There are a number of targets on the agenda and I believe that these are designated as part of the negotiation plan as being the optimum outcome: what your real target actually is and what your settlement point might be (what you will accept worse-case scenario prior to walking away [exit point]). This is shown in Figure 5.1.

Figure 5.1 is pretty self-explanatory, but I would draw the reader's attention to the fact that there are interfaces between the different levels, that is, there will be degrees of achievement within the different bands shown. For instance, an agreement may be reached

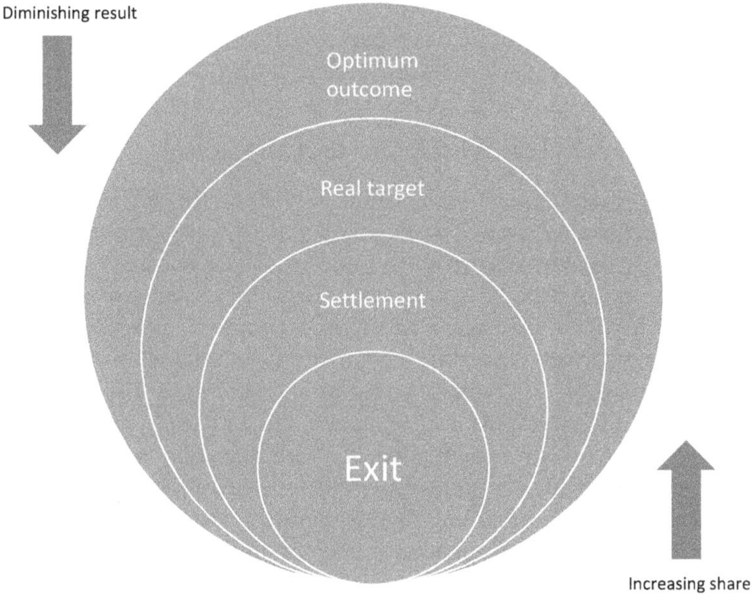

Figure 5.1 The Competitive Negotiation Linear Process Model.

between Settlement and Real Target. To contextualise this, imagine that you were prepared as a settlement to accept anything between the range of £300,000 and £400,000 with your Real Target being between the range of £500,000 and £700,000 and the deal is struck at £600,000. This is not the optimum that you were trying for (perhaps unrealistically depending on many factors and variables) and is representative of the midpoint of what you were really looking for, so I would view it as a definite positive outcome. A big issue here is that the other party might also view this as a positive outcome and feel that you have been reasonable. A win/win situation! Note: the exit point has no range. As soon as you reach this zone, you should walk away. There is no point in prolonging the process any further.

Disadvantages of this style:

1 Irreparably damage longer-term/future relationships
2 Become very emotive, detracts from purpose of negotiation, cranks up the stress level, causes focus to change
3 Perceived outcomes often overly optimistic

4 Compliance with agreement may be difficult to manage/oversee
5 Kills any creativity between parties (i.e. jointly looking to overcome issues)

THE CO-OPERATIVE STYLE OF NEGOTIATION

Generally speaking, the intent with this stylistic approach is to ensure that there are no losers. The key to making the co-operative style work is for the counterparties to understand one another's position right at the outset. A good way to achieve this is to have pre-negotiation meetings to agree on a comprehensive agenda of issues desired to be settled by both parties (when I say settled, I'm not suggesting as in a dispute resolution, but rather points to be negotiated). This can become a streamlined and very efficient process, *if* both parties are playing straight with one another and there is no deception going on (unfortunately this is a counter-crux, the big potential weakness of attempting to operate within this manner). In the case where no such agenda has been ratified between the parties, then success utilising this style of negotiation will revolve around flexibility and being able to adapt your position as events unfold (this should always be the case anyway). The co-operative style is about generating options, exploring different paths as to how agreement may be reached and the achievement of a mutually beneficial and desirable outcome.

The author believes that the co-operative style is best suited when there are multiple objectives to be achieved and it is not immediately apparent what this is going to look like, hence the co-operation between the counterparties. It is evident then, that for this approach to work, there has to be a sharing of information to enable collaboration towards a mutually beneficial outcome. As I have mentioned throughout, part of the essence of a successful negotiated result is the ability to 'horse trade.' Everyone has a different perspective and the two sides around the table will be no exception. If you can discover (either mutually through working together or just from your side) an objective that might be relatively important to the counterparty but isn't really to you, then this is good leverage for first achieving something in return that may be vice versa and second for enhancing the positivity of the proceedings as everyone seems to be getting what they want.

Disadvantages:

1 Making unnecessary compromises
2 More exposed/vulnerable to deception/manipulation by other parties if they are not playing straight
3 Can be difficult to ascertain best outcome between parties
4 Over-reliance on negotiator's perception of other party's position and agenda

In my live negotiation programme, one of the exercises that I get members of the class to perform is what I call The Ultimatum Game. The purpose of this game is to demonstrate the results when utilising either the competitive or co-operative style of negotiation. Eight out of ten times, the results are nearly always the same. I've run this game over a lot of programmes around the world, so it's interesting that it seems to transcend even national and organisational cultural behaviour and the gender role seems irrelevant.

In this game, a control party negotiates with multiple parties. The control party has all the power and this is known to all participants: that they are at an immediate disadvantage, but should seek to obtain the best result that they can. There are multiple objectives to be achieved; each is assigned a monetary value. Some of the teams are briefed on taking a competitive approach – staying strong and being hard – pushing to maximise their gains, being intractable, bluffing and generally being more aggressive. Some of the other teams are briefed to follow a co-operative style – seeking to find and explore options – looking for collaboration with the control party. I don't think that the reader will be overly surprised to be told that the latter group outperforms the former group (in most cases) substantially in terms of revenue made. It is always interesting to me to watch this dynamic and in the debrief listen to the feedback from the participants. Often, the control group will report that they simply became offended or didn't like the aggressive teams, so were not really interested in doing any deals, particularly over the longer term. In contrast, positive feelings seemed to be generated by a mutually co-operative approach. Occasionally, of course, the competitive teams would make a big win, probably due to being more composed and better actors. However, they knew (and participants expressed this) that this approach tended towards a 'take it now and who cares about the future.' Negotiation is a dynamic process, and whilst there is a lot of value in pondering the exercise above, it is important to remember that the styles of the counterparties can oscillate between the two as facts unfold during a singular negotiation. Prior to commencement, the author suggests that the reader consider what I think are the key criteria to making your choice – at least as to how you wish to begin the proceedings, given below:

1 Consider and evaluate what the purpose of the negotiation is
2 Clarify your objectives and goals
3 Consider the relationship angle
4 Determine likely risk profile, that is, possible outcomes and their ramifications, on what choice you make on how to negotiate
5 How much time do you have?
6 Assess any financial implications – impact of choice

Silver Bullet: There are advantages and disadvantages to any negotiation style. Understand that you must be capable of harvesting the benefits of a particular approach on a case-by-case basis. All negotiations are unique.

In addition to the six key factors listed above, I would suggest that some further preparatory evaluation should be done by considering some other complimentary, important factors in conjunction. It is important to know what the level of the forthcoming negotiation is: What's at stake? What does this negotiation mean for our organisation, for our competitive advantage, for our longevity as a corporate entity? Is this a strategic negotiation (questions posed above)? Is it a tactical negotiation? Are we executing our plan towards achieving our strategic mission and vision to facilitate the big questions listed above? Or is this an operational negotiation (repetitive and relatively frequent, that is, procurement/supplier contracts)? You should evaluate how thorough your due diligence procedure has been: How informed you are about the counterparties? How well do you understand the subject matter and related issues and their ramifications to the upcoming negotiation? Is the scope of the negotiation clearly defined? Do we know what's 'on the table' and what's 'off the table?' Have we identified those issues (mentioned earlier) that we are prepared to burn off (i.e. of relatively low importance to our position, but good leverage with counterparties' position? Last, and perhaps of vital importance, do you have a clearly defined exit point? Is there a time when you must simply quit and walk away from the table? (see Competitive Negotiation Linear Process Model). I want to share a simple example with you about exit points. It is not a commercial example, but I feel it is the most powerful one to illustrate and underline the importance of the principle. You are on holiday and decide that you have £500 budget for gambling in the local casino. Your run of luck seems to have deserted you and you are down to £200. Common sense tells you that you should cut your losses and put it down to experience. After all, £200 could go back into the 'holiday pot'. Perhaps you could buy the kids something nice. But then, the counterargument begins to assert itself. You are on holiday, how often do you get the chance to gamble? Potentially, you could turn your £500 into £5,000. Imagine the benefits of that! This line of reasoning is very persuasive – you stay at the poker table. A short while later your £200 is gone. This is another exit point. But you are angered now, you are in a decision fatigue state. It's been a long night and earlier euphoria has worn off. Emotions are ruling you, you are not being objective. You cash another £500 – you're going to win no matter what! You start to place bigger bets, you win some, but ultimately you end up bankrupt, your extra investment producing nothing. You also realise that the extra expenditure will reduce what was planned in terms of holiday activities for the family. You have failed yourself and your family. You did not have a clearly defined exit point and paid the price for 'staying at the table.' I have seen this in casinos and I've seen it around the boardroom table – it's a cautionary tale.

6

PLANNING TO NEGOTIATE

To be truly effective at negotiation, the author believes that you have to inherently understand the 'Three Ps Pyramid Model' given in Figure 6.1.

THE THREE PS PYRAMID MODEL

There are three rules you must know:

1 Understand the Process
2 Know the People
3 Master the Psychology

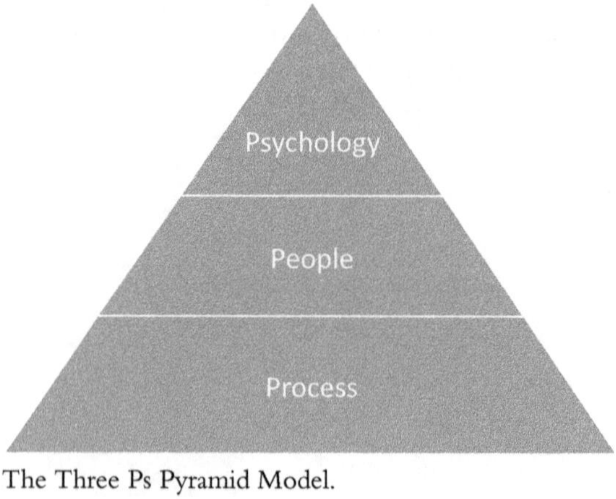

Figure 6.1 The Three Ps Pyramid Model.

DOI: 10.4324/9781003263722-6

The reason why this model is a pyramid carries great significance (in my mind) of the relative share of the negotiation planning process. As can be seen, the base of the pyramid (which represents the biggest component) is all about the process – this is the evaluation and planning pre-negotiation. This is understanding the mechanics and the interrelationships between impacting and important factors (e.g. agenda and time management). The mid-tier represents the involved parties and other stakeholders – who they are and what is their relative importance to the process. The apex of the pyramid deals with perhaps the hardest component of negotiation – the psychology. I would suggest to you that as well as many other things, negotiation is all about psychology. Psychology governs the way people think and their behaviour and value systems. Master the psychology (both your own and that of others) and you will find that you are an elite-level negotiator. Psychology is the ever-present intangible that creates the tangible results; therefore, a commercial negotiation is, in essence, a reification.

Quite often the goals and desired outcomes to a commercial negotiation are not precisely clear. This often occurs due to a range of factors: miscommunications, misunderstandings of fact (i.e. misinterpretation of documentary issues/facts), assumptions made that prove erroneous and the dichotomy between personal and corporate perception. To further complicate the issue, the ultimate outcome of any negotiation, with the best will in the world, is unknown (unless you can see into the future, which would render any need to negotiate with anyone defunct). Any negotiation will always have one or a few core critical elements in terms of 'the heart of the matter.' This is where the focus should primarily be but is often not as the process gets side-tracked by peripheral issues that lead off on a tangent (sometimes quite a significant tangent). When planning to negotiate, *focus* on what you are doing, why you are doing it and what is the purpose (i.e. what are you trying/wanting to achieve)? It is imperative to clearly define the scope of the upcoming proceedings to avoid 'ground clutter,' to prevent the process from being sidetracked unnecessarily and to maximise the uptake efficiency in both time and process management.

I have always found it useful, when commencing my negotiation planning, to take a step back before I begin and to 'look behind' the obvious. At the core or the heart of the matter, there will exist a rationale for why this negotiation is going to occur, regardless of any other facts. If you truly, concisely and with absolute clarity understand WHY this negotiation is going to happen, then you will have both precision and clarity in structuring your agenda for the procedure to come. It's not simply because you've been told to 'get round the table and bring us home something good,' it's not obeying orders, nor is it 'I'm a negotiator. I negotiate' (playing a role as an actor on a stage). It's about extrapolation, harnessing your personal and organisational knowledge, your learning and experience to date. It's about trying to envision an end state, a post-negotiation outcome and the benefits that it will provide and accrue in the future and the reasons why this will be so. I have often thought that a good way to envision a negotiation plan is to consider it as the backbone of your plans and agenda. To run with this analogy, it is central and runs through the entire process. It is your strength and support, yet it is flexible and can change direction, it consists of different sized components, each of which has a role to play and a function to perform.

The Triple C Model in Figure 6.2 is how I always check (either alone if operating solo or with the team) the veracity of the planning process that is underway. As the reader can see, this is a cyclical model and the process is ongoing throughout the planning phase.

The cycle is divided into three segments and the reader will notice that they are of equal size, denoting their equal importance to both one another and to the cycle in itself. The author believes that adherence to this model during the planning phase will reap significant benefits to those who utilise it.

THE TRIPLE C MODEL

When using this model, you could start from any given segment and work around it from there. I, however, always begin with the 'communication' segment. The author has always found that having the right conversation from the start with whoever is involved ensures the greatest amount of clarity in planning. This applies across the stakeholder continuum – it might be senior management within your organisation who are 'tasking' you to perform the negotiation, it might be colleagues who are going to be part of the negotiation team or, in the case of a collaborative endeavour such as a JV, it

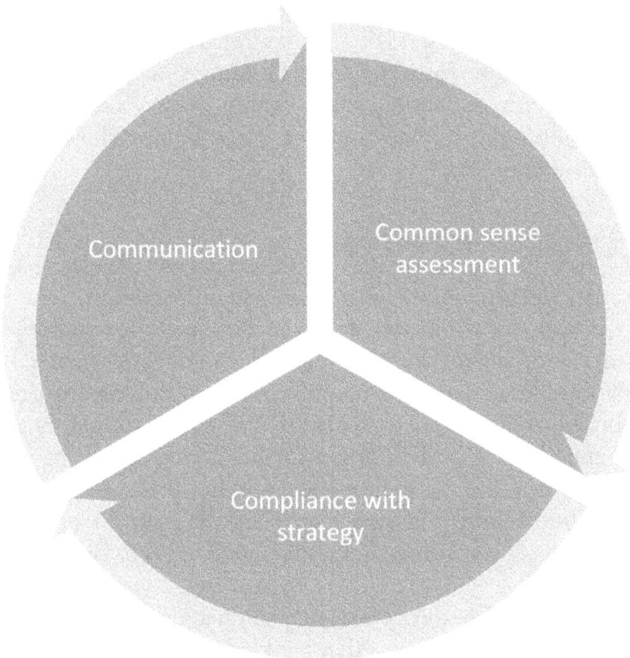

Figure 6.2 The Triple C Model.

might even be members of the counterparty (consider conversation earlier regarding co-operative styles of negotiation). Regardless of who it might be, knowing what everyone's expectations are is the best foundation you could lay. Moving on from this, I like to then ratify what I know and have learnt through the communication process and apply a common-sense assessment. This is where you can check assumptions and the feasibility of expectations: assess what will or will not work. This moves you into the next segment of the model and serves as a double enforcer. Many of the facts that you have gleaned from the communication and assessment stages will serve as clear pointers as to their fit with the strategy that you are planning to execute. You may well discover during this phase of the process that there is an inconsistency, or something is unrealistic in terms of the strategy to be deployed that you could place yourself at some disadvantage. This then allows you to re-engage within the communication segment, and so the cycle continues. The author would suggest to the reader that this model is worth keeping 'live' during the entire process of the negotiation as it will provide a comprehensive method of assessing current status within the proceedings (i.e. in a longer negotiation, review against the day's occurrences, in a short negotiation; perhaps make a quick review during a break, such as at lunchtime).

THE DUE DILIGENCE PROCESS

All human decision-making is based on information. The better informed you are, the better decisions you make (or should) about key issues and sub-issues. The purpose of collecting and collating information, of leaving no stone unturned and finding any skeletons in cupboards is ultimately to be aware and not be caught by surprise around the table. Good information helps to define and establish your risk profile for the pending negotiation (consideration of factors and options and outcome scenarios). The author believes that there are two classifications of due diligence (DD) information: hard and soft.

Hard information – things that are quantifiable are real – commercial and environmental facts, facts that are known and can be objectively proven. Soft information, however, is more subjective and difficult to prove. This is information relative to the counterparty's psychological makeup, their attitude/temperament and how they reason. This is why the Three Ps Pyramid Model is so useful. The process mainly consists of hard information; the people are representative of both hard and soft information, whilst the psychology at the apex is soft information. Remember though that not all information is of the same quality relevant to your needs and that information in itself often has a 'shelf life' (i.e. it will be valuable for a period of time, after which it will carry either no value or a very diminished one). Information has different values at different times to different people. It is imperative that the commercial negotiator understands this and checks the information upon which the plan is based for relevance, precision and value as well as making a consideration as to what information the counterparty may possess or have access to that differentiates their position from yours. As food for thought, consider the Silver Bullet below.

Silver Bullet: 'The further into the future that you are planning for, the greater the uncertainty – the greater the uncertainty, the greater the risk – the greater the risk, the greater the reward.'

From the strategic level of negotiation, the statement above encapsulates what I believe drives some individuals during these high-stake procedures. The reader may recall an earlier discussion within this book about the 'overarching risk strategies.' My point being that no matter what the risk analysis may say, no matter how detailed, there is still ultimately a human being who is the final arbiter in terms of any decision made and that decision will ultimately be expressed in terms of the decision makers' attitude to risk.

Silver Bullet: Information has great relevance to negotiation – it may bring to light potential pitfalls and traps or reveal a hidden danger in pursuing a particular strategy and will therefore have a direct role in shaping a focussed negotiation plan and strategy, one that will be the most efficient in terms of cost and time management.

The list below encapsulates what I think are the main benefits of detailed planning:

- Less likely to be 'caught unaware'
- More streamlined and efficient negotiation process – you know what you are trying to achieve
- Less chance of 'splitting hairs' – more clarity in what is agreed
- Closer alignment between objectives and achievements
- Knowledge of competitors and their behaviour
- The current operating environment
- Factors that could negatively impact – substitutes?
- Any relevant cost/financial information

7

PREPARING TO NEGOTIATE

The author feels that there is often an inconsistency in people's minds between 'planning' to negotiate and 'preparing' to negotiate. They should be viewed (in my opinion) as two sides of the same coin, as representing a logical progression. I have always considered planning as the establishment of the broad framework: the identification of goals and objectives, the evaluation of information and the setting of the agenda. Preparation, however, is the fine honing of that framework by the consideration of the operational realities and what bearing they may have on the execution of the strategy and plan. The seven key steps given below is a template that I developed many years ago and I still use it every time as the framework guide for my negotiation preparation. It works and serves to ensure you have not omitted or forgotten something important in your preparations.

THE SEVEN KEY STEPS FOR NEGOTIATION PREPARATION

1 Analyse identified scenarios for advantages and disadvantages.
2 Is there anything that is a priority for us to achieve?
3 What is our trade-off tolerance?
4 Decide on the overall approach/conduct of the negotiation.
5 Formalise your strategy.
6 Review plans and strategy.
7 Create 'live' agenda prior to commencement.

DOI: 10.4324/9781003263722-7

A critical point within the preparation process for me has always been consideration of where the negotiation is going to be held. This is very important for a number of reasons and there are a number of connotations that have to be considered. There are obviously only three possibilities: on home ground, on the counterparty's ground or somewhere neutral. Often, if a negotiation is going to occur at one of the party's offices, then this is an indication of the relative power of the parties, as a home environment conveys an immediate psychological advantage over the counterparty – it is your ground, not theirs. In an earlier chapter, we discussed the various styles adopted by negotiators, and as the reader may recall, the co-operative approach was in most cases more beneficial for longer-term relationships. If this approach is being taken (co-operative), then it is not uncommon for both sides to make their first concession very early. Let's conduct the proceedings in a neutral venue where there is no advantage to either party in terms of home ground.

The next element that I feel is very important is to consider the actual physical features of where the negotiation is going to take place. This is where the subtle tricks are employed, of which there are quite a number, all geared towards acquiring a tactical advantage, especially if on home ground. A good starting point is to consider the seating arrangements. This may sound innocuous. Believe me it is anything but! There is great value in knowing these things, from the perspective of being either the host or the visitor. A common tactic is to arrange the seating such that the counterparty is facing the window looking at your team, who is sitting with their back to it looking into the room. The brighter the day outside, the greater this advantage. I won't belabour the point. I'm sure we have all had a conversation with someone who was silhouetted against a bright sky – it becomes very difficult to see their faces! Beware, though, of having this seating arrangement after dark if there are no curtains or blinds drawn. The party looking outwards may well have an additional view of your side of the table through the reflection (situation dependent, of course) in the windows. The author was once at a negotiation where we were able to see the counterparties nudging each other at times and even passing a note across under the table, believing it was out of sight. Another ploy associated with seating is to ensure that one set of seats are lower than the other. If you are looking up, even slightly, it subconsciously conveys a lesser status; you feel at a disadvantage and possibly uncomfortable. One of my personal favourites is to spend as much time as possible standing when addressing a counterparty. I sometimes mask it as being respectful or polite, but I know that I have the advantage of looking down. This is magnified if you are able to pace whilst talking, perhaps using a whiteboard as pretence. Nothing influences and reinforces a point better than walking directly up to someone or leaning over the back of your chair towards them while speaking, then moving away again, probably accompanied by a gesture or two (consider points raised in the chapter on non-verbal communication). The way the seating is physically deployed is another deliberate strategy. If you are operating solo and are facing a team of negotiators, it is not uncommon to place the seats in a 'C' shape around your seat and unobtrusively spaced out. The reason for this is that from your seat, you cannot simultaneously see all the other individuals – you have to turn your head. When you can't see all the people you're talking to, you are at a disadvantage as you might miss vital, subtle nuances as to intention and truth. This particular ploy though is a bit of a toothless tiger if you're aware of it, as it is very easily countered. It happened to me a while ago. When I walked into the room and saw this seating configuration, it made me smile. It works on the basis of you not wanting to make a scene and to sit where indicated. I simply picked up the chair (I was facing three in the 'C') and moved it back until I could clearly see everyone. This obviously annoyed one of the hosts as they asked me rather indignantly what I was doing. I smiled easily and pointed out that I couldn't see everyone at the original distance. They could hardly say that that was a deliberate ploy on their part. I was just being helpful, ensuring that we all got the most from the proceedings. The last point I want to make relative to seating is that of comfort. This can work both ways – again, depending on your role within a situation. Hard, uncomfortable seats (particularly in a hot room) soon become a distraction in themselves, as people grow increasingly irksome with their discomfort. The opposite is also true – super comfy seating can actually make tired people more tired, as they subconsciously react to the comfort encapsulating their weary bodies. There are various ways to play the comfort dimension: uncomfortable seating for fresh counterparties and comfortable seating for tired counterparties, who have perhaps had a long flight or journey to reach you or you know were burning the midnight oil getting ready, to be used in conjunction with setting the room temperature to warm or even hot and deciding upon an appropriate lighting level. Anyone who has ever sat through protracted, complex negotiations will know precisely what a big impact these small refinements can make to both the process and the outcome.

I have indicated that both temperature and lighting are important as well and feel that the reader will understand the ramifications of how these can be used in conjunction with actual seating. Other important facets of the physical negotiation environment are issues such as privacy: Is there anywhere to have a 'time out' to discuss something in private? Are there toilet facilities? A common tactic here is to ensure that the nearest toilets are a good few minutes' walk away – this interrupts any flow (no pun intended!) and might provide a party with an opportunity for a quick conflab out of sight or earshot. The provision (or not) of refreshments is another tool that can be used. If none are provided (particularly considering some of the points discussed thus far), then this in itself becomes a distraction as individuals become thirsty or hungry. Their intention increasingly turns towards pondering how much longer until a break and where they may be able to find something to drink or a snack; there is therefore a loss of focus, a distraction. Conversely, a generous level of refreshments can have several connotations from appearing to be a munificent host to ensuring that refreshments are in the opposite direction to the toilets (this is one I've seen more than I care to remember!).

The author was once involved within a negotiation that took place in the basement of the counterparty's offices. It was remote and isolated (to ensure the utmost privacy apparently due to the 'highly sensitive nature' of the talks taking place!). Access was down several flights of stairs. There were no windows and the lighting was excessively bright and glaring. The room was hot. The toilets and refreshments were back up the stairs. The seating was uncomfortable – our seats were directly in front of the central heating panels that mysteriously appeared to be turned up very high, judging from the heat radiating out from them that soon had us all in shirtsleeves. There was no Wi-Fi and no phone signal. Every time anyone wanted to make a call, it was a merry trek up the stairs again. As the first day wore on, the process became increasingly fragmented due to people needing to use the bathroom, make calls or simply stretch their aching bodies and get some fresh air. I have no doubt that these tactics would've been successful, at least in part, had this particular negotiation been just for a single day; however, given the scope of the proceedings, expectations were that it would be at least three days, if not five to eight. It was fortunate that both parties were reasonably well balanced in the equation.

This backfired on the counterparty as we insisted on moving the location for the subsequent days and we got to choose a neutral location, which was, in fact, a hotel that we had close ties to as we used it a lot and were on good terms with many of the staff. I believe that this rather extreme example shows that you can't overdo the tricks and tactics as it might become counterproductive (as in this case) or could have even possibly have derailed the entire process (the author believes that if the counterparty had not agreed to move location, we would've chosen this as an exit point as we had other possible options in signing a similar deal with other parties).

Silver Bullet: The physical aspects to a negotiation environment represent tools of manipulation: seating, lighting, privacy, toilets, refreshments, Wi-Fi availability and telecoms can all be used in a variety of ways in order to influence both the proceedings and the outcome of a commercial negotiation.

When preparing for an upcoming negotiation, I believe that the points below serve as a useful final run through and check list of your planning. I have used this list many times prior to commencement the following day or a few days beforehand.

Mission objectives:

1 What are our goals and aims?
2 What are we trying to achieve?
3 What is our settlement point?
4 Is there an exit strategy/potential (i.e. is there a point where we will walk away)?
5 What is our relative power position?
6 What time constraints do we have?

Silver Bullet: Never underestimate the importance of preparation in commercial negotiations – nothing is as crucial for achieving a successful outcome.

8

DECISION-MAKING WITHIN NEGOTIATION SCENARIOS

Decision-making is yet another of the intangible, seemingly abstract, aspects of negotiating with other people, and sometimes it makes me smile to think that there are so many elements to the process that if you looked – you couldn't actually see or touch, coupled with the fact that the process is uncertain and the outcome is unknown. It almost seems a fool's errand.

Intangible or not though, the decision-making process leads to the manifestation of tangible things: deals are struck, agreements are made, wheels are set in motion. I think that this is the 'magic' of negotiation – that something can come from nothing. The quantum of resultant benefits, I believe, is a mirror reflection of the skill of the negotiator(s). In a previous chapter, the value of information was discussed, and the statement made that the better information you had, the better informed you were and therefore logically progressing towards making better decisions.

Once you have performed the due diligence process, looked under every rock and in every cupboard – you need to organise the information into building scenarios. A safe methodology for doing this is to construct three distinct stories (scenarios): one where everything goes just perfect and you get everything you want (optimistic scenario), the most likely way things will play out (realistic scenario) and the version where the worst possible outcome materialises (the pessimistic scenario). By doing this, you are casting your net as wide as possible to attempt to foresee how things might transpire – therefore being prepared and not being taken by surprise and being able to adapt. Scenarios should be anticipatory, containing both reactive and proactive dimensions.

DOI: 10.4324/9781003263722-8

Additionally, when constructing scenarios, the author believes that there are a few further key considerations that should also be taken into account as to what their (likely) impact might be on proceedings. For me, a good starting point is to evaluate any potential cultural differences that could arise, especially from mistakes and blunders perpetrated through stupidity. I have seen numerous occasions where simple blunders have derailed a process completely, simply through ignorance causing grievous offence. When negotiating internationally, you are by default negotiating cross-culturally. Different cultures have different beliefs, values and behavioural norms. The author has seen this when international organisations fail to grasp that the establishment of a localised Strategic Business Unit (SBU) might be better off on a decentralised basis (i.e. operating autonomy) to cope with local conditions and regulations (i.e. local content issues) rather than a prescriptive operating blueprint from the headquarters (HQ), which, in effect, becomes a straitjacket.

Given the comment above about scenarios being anticipatory and containing both proactive and reactive elements, this is better understood if the reader, upon completing their scenarios, attempts to estimate the 'drift' that may (or is likely) to occur during the negotiation proceedings. By drift I mean the departure from expected outcomes. The degree of magnitude of drift will be a key determinant as to what scenario you might find yourself within (i.e. things are going badly and are well off the mark – this is your pessimistic case – look to it for evaluation of the present circumstances in terms of what can be addressed from an improvement/rectification perspective). What did you anticipate in this scenario? Another important element to the efficiency of any scenarios that have been generated to inform the decision-making process is to evaluate what I call the 'range tolerances.' Earlier in the book, the author discussed the idea of 'trade-off' and how something that is not of particular importance to you might actually be important to the counterparty and vice versa. I also discussed 'burn off' – what you are prepared to lose in order to gain something (remember both trade-off and burn off are not necessarily financial considerations, they could be intangibles such as goodwill or longer-term relationship considerations).

The author believes that there are two important decision-making nexuses within commercial negotiations: two 'crossroads' that like it or not and the important decisions that must be made.

The first of these is your 'settlement point' (SP). This is what you will accept in terms of a fair deal. It is basically the last bastion before the second of the two nexuses – the 'exit point' (EP) – the point at which, come what may, you walk away from the table. If your SP is not unduly onerous or unrealistic, then this becomes your 'safety stop' where the outcome is not viewed as being disadvantageous to your position. It's not great, but it's acceptable. The EP, however, represents a failure in terms of achieving any outcome whatsoever. This result may stem from a plethora of factors, some if not many that are totally out of your control. A wise man knows when it's time to walk away.

There are other factors that will dictate the arrival at either of the two nexuses mentioned above. Often, the number of open options can give cause for re-evaluation of the present situation. Of course, if you have arrived at the EP, then it is likely that all reasonable options have been exhausted. At the SP, however, it might be time to change the game plan and consider pursuing a slightly different strategy. It is important to understand the future ramifications of decisions made in the present. I would go so far as to express my opinion that this is the most important evaluation to make within any given decision-making process. In a previous chapter, the author made the statement that 'the further into the future decisions are being made for, the greater the uncertainty and therefore the greater the risk and ultimately the greater the reward.' In the longer term, the risk level is always higher (and I believe that this is exponential) as it is impossible to know some future state or outcome, and the further away or greater the time frame, then there is more uncertainty in terms of variables that might impact, for instance, if negotiating a Joint Venture (JV) Agreement, key stakeholders might change as might resource requirements or even operating methodologies. Who, for instance, would've predicted the outbreak of COVID-19 and its impacts? Consider how this would've changed many a negotiation strategy, or perhaps nullified any intent/interest in negotiating a particular deal.

The difficulty with short-term decision-making is precisely that the longer term represents the unknown and is unquantifiable, so decisions that are taken in the present might have a negative impact on some future state. This is further compounded by human behaviour. Often, when under pressure, decision makers operate from a knee-jerk perspective – if they can make the problem go away, at least for the immediate term, then this is fine. The idea of 'crossing bridges when you get to them' is alive and well within the corporate world of today – believe me. But this is not an optimal solution for making decisions that prove robust and resilient (as far as is possible). Some time ago, I created a simple mnemonic model when attempting to address this sort of problem. I call it the Problem Acceptable in the Short Term (PAST) model. The idea behind this model is to attempt to alleviate this mindset and approach and not to seek short-term issues or ignore a problem 'for now'. The common causes whereby negotiators fall into the PAST trap tend to revolve around ill-thought-out, trade-off, decision-making processes, conceding too much to attempt to persuade/satisfy or incentivise powerful stakeholders and counterparties, delaying decisions and attempting to alter the negotiation strategy in order to rework something without careful consideration.

The modern corporate entity operates in an environment that is turbulent, to say the least. The quest for creating and maintaining a competitive advantage that is sustainable is a significant marker in any strategic level decision-making processes. Change is inevitable, but the author believes that even if the organisation recognises this, it must react in the correct way. If it changes too fast, it becomes something else, something different. This may alienate its core customer base, leading ultimately to failure. Conversely though, the organisation that changes too slowly will be left behind by its competitors – will ultimately ossify and die. This challenge is central to the corporate decision maker and to the negotiator who is trying to realise the way forward for the organisation's future.

The author has noticed during his time as a consultant and negotiator specialist that there is often a serious disconnect between corporate and operational levels within organisations. This has always been one of the great corporate mysteries to me, as I have never quite been able to fathom why different organisational components don't want to invest some time (probably nothing onerous in reality) in communicating with one another. This causes what I call an 'organisational tension' as the corporate level decision makers set policy and strategic goals, yet often don't seem to understand that these desires are disconnected from the operational reality. For the commercial negotiator, I believe that there is nothing worse than being tasked to achieve the impossible. A lot of senior organisational figures, in the author's experience, have forgotten that there's no point in being a general if you don't have an army. Not understanding output capacities, resource levels, lead times and project initiatives properly is anathema to me when I realise that I am dealing with individuals who are not fully informed as to their organisation's actual capabilities. 'Nice to have' is not always a good cornerstone of strategic desire. The role of organisational politics and power dispersion throughout the organisation are often regrettably major drivers of both policy and decision-making processes.

Silver Bullet: Decision-making should always obey three core rules: clarity in its objectives, realism in terms of organisational capabilities and precision in its planning and execution.

NEGOTIATION AS A TOOL FOR DISPUTE RESOLUTION

When parties meet around the negotiation table, I often wonder how much thought is given to any negative consequences that might arise at some future point. As mentioned in the preceding chapter, decisions taken in the short term are often incompatible with some future state. But this is only one element of the issue. Disputes can erupt around the table during the negotiation process, often as a result of misunderstandings, poor communication and emotive responses taking over.

The author believes that if individuals were completely candid, then no one wants to find themselves engaged within a dispute, no matter the reason or the magnitude. As discussed in Chapter 4, there are many costs associated with the manifestation of conflict, and these are at best counterproductive whilst at worst lead to litigation or formal arbitration, resulting in significant costs.

Negotiation as a process though (outwith the contractual dimension) is a very useful tool for resolving disputes. Those of us engaged within the Alternative Dispute Resolution (ADR) industry often utilise a 'ladder' methodology of process and the first two rungs of this are normally negotiation, split into informal and formal proceedings. The idea behind the ladder concept is that the sooner a dispute can be resolved and settled, the less disruption caused and the fewer costs involved.

Formal negotiations, if utilised for dispute resolution, are normally very structured. There is a defined agenda worked up and agreed by the parties to the dispute as to what will be discussed/negotiated. There will be an agreed location and time. The individuals involved will be identified as will any agents who may have a

DOI: 10.4324/9781003263722-9

role of some sort in the proceedings. The elements and sub-elements of the agenda will be worked through in an agreed sequence to a timetable. If the intention of the parties by utilising formal negotiation is to try to prevent any escalation further up the dispute ladder (i.e. arbitration) but it is uncertain whether an agreement will be reached, then there will often be a clock running on the negotiations which will set a time frame for resolution to be achieved (e.g. the negotiation will take place w/c 'X' for three days at location 'Y'). This mechanism therefore puts an emphasis on the participants to utilise the time as efficiently as possible towards achieving a resolution (hopefully a positive one).

Although it might seem to the reader to be back-to-front, sometimes informal negotiations can be more effective than the process described above. I am a great believer that if it is possible to resolve your differences in an informal manner, it could actually have a positive longer-term effect, but is obviously dependent upon a number of factors. The pertinent question then is why? Why should an unstructured process that has no kind of control mechanism be more effective than something that is precisely defined, structured and organised? The answer is simplicity itself – people may know each other within a different context and this allows problems to be resolved in a more relaxed manner that is not constrained or defined by some sort of prescriptive procedure. Consider, for example, a junior executive whose uncle happens to be a major shareholder within the organisation or is married to the CEO's niece. Perhaps people are members of the same club and have a shared passion. If these sorts of informal relationships exist, they are often effective because of the different context – people may be more attentive and apt to listen whilst feeling relaxed and rested. Often, organisational social conventions may be disregarded or negated in this manner. If such informal relationships exist, I would very strongly urge the reader to make use of them. They are often very effective at resolving things; one way or the other, the resolution can be quicker and this often has cost-saving implications.

Another very effective negotiation-based strategy of resolving disputes whilst avoiding the more costly, formal mechanisms such as arbitration is to establish a dispute resolution board early on. These have been utilised within the civil engineering construction industry for many years and appear to have been very successful. I believe the reason for the success of this mode is that it offers a structured approach through simplicity and common sense. Generally speaking, three individuals are selected/volunteer to sit on the board. They tend to be a representative of each of the parties, with one member being a neutral. This ensures that decisions will either be unanimous or 2 to 1. Dispute boards then are incapable of ending up in deadlock, so therefore a decision is a guaranteed outcome. The board only convenes once a dispute arises between the parties. Everyone gets to present their case and make their arguments. The dispute board will make a ruling. It is important to note though that the ruling is really a recommendation and carries no legal binding obligations. What the author has always found interesting though is that the parties, having had their say and listening to both the position of the counterparty and the advice from the board, seem (quite often) to bring about a settlement through compromise and often build better relationships between the parties going forward.

The use of mediation as a dispute negotiation mechanism seems to be growing more popular. The idea of a mediator might be thought of as the appointment by both parties of a proxy negotiator who familiarises themselves with both viewpoints. Mediation seems to be the vehicle of choice where a situation arises that the parties are no longer willing to deal or communicate face to face with one another. A mediator should be considered an impartial influencer; they listen to both sides of the dispute, probing, asking questions and clarifying issues. Misunderstandings/miscommunications often come to light, and this frequently paves the way for some kind of settlement or agreement between the parties. Just like the dispute boards mentioned above, it must be remembered that the parties are not bound in any way to accept or listen to any of the recommendations that are made by the mediator. Mediation can often represent a quick and cost-effective solution, but not without the participation and willingness to listen and negotiate between the parties.

Fairly recently, newer ideas have emerged, I believe with the intention of still not wanting to progress up the ladder of ADR (i.e. increasing cost/time and formality), if at all possible. One such hybrid approach is known as 'Med-Arb' – this is what it says on the tin – a combined approach utilising mediation initially, progressing onwards to a full-blown arbitration to deal with any unresolved issues. The intention, therefore, of the parties is to hopefully settle most, if not all, issues at the mediation phase as opposed to moving onwards to the arbitration. This approach is becoming increasingly popular, as it provides this element of flexibility to the parties who may want to try to settle issues earlier (and cheaper) but are prepared to enter into more costly and time-consuming mechanisms such as formal arbitration if it becomes necessary.

Arb-Med is another approach that almost seems opposite to the one discussed above. The main feature of this idea is that an arbitrator engages in the arbitral process but makes an almost advisory decision (award) that is non-binding. It is akin to getting an opinion or a recommendation given to the parties. This opinion of the arbitrator is then used as the basis for a mediation.

When counterparties sit down at the negotiation table, there is (or most definitely should be) an awareness that over time, as a commercial contract is being performed, it is a very real possibility that disputes of some manner or form will arise. Even though the purpose of negotiating a tight commercial contract that attempts to capture all rights, duties and obligations of the parties is ideal, it is still impossible to accurately gauge every component of some future state or operating environment. It is now commonplace to ensure that every commercial contract contains a dispute resolution or an arbitral clause. The inclusion of an arbitral clause provides a mechanism to which the parties have agreed will govern the resolution process of a dispute, should one arise. This therefore provides certainty to the parties as the way forward should they find themselves in this situation. In the author's opinion, there are two major advantages to the inclusion of the arbitral clause: escalation abilities (if drafted and agreed thus) and the Doctrine of Separability.

An escalative arbitral clause (aka a multi-tiered arbitral clause, mentioned at the start of the chapter) is one that contains elements of the dispute resolution ladder. The idea is that the parties specify several steps or stages (tiers) when attempting to resolve their differences. So, it may be agreed and prescribed that in the event of a dispute, the parties will initially attempt formal negotiation; if this fails, they will move onto mediation, and if this fails, they will go to a formal arbitration (as a singular example). What is important to understand about an escalative clause is that the parties must go through all the stages (tiers) in sequence. If, for example, one of the parties wanted to ignore the earlier steps and go straight to arbitration, this would not be allowed. Any number of dispute resolution methodologies can be included. Simply put, the rationale behind having a multi-tiered (escalative) arbitral clause is that the parties try to resolve the dispute as quickly and cost-effectively as possible. This also creates a solid framework as to the actions required in the event of a dispute and, as stated, the process cannot be circumvented by the parties.

The Doctrine of Separability is an important thing to be aware of. Outside of the legal field, I believe few people have any idea as to what it is or its importance. What it means is simply this – if a contract fails (void due to illegality or becomes void due to lack of performance), the arbitral clause remains alive and arbitration proceedings may still be brought in terms of the agreed arbitral clause in the contract against the counterparties. Normally, the main argument that might have the effect of nullifying the arbitral clause is that of public policy.

This chapter serves to illustrate the pervasive nature of negotiation within the world of commerce and the many different ways in which it plays a central role in the resolution of disputes. There are obviously advantages and disadvantages associated with the different methodologies that might be adopted, but I believe that these can be easily encapsulated in terms of cost, time, enforceability (therefore certainty) and implications for relationships.

Silver Bullet: Care and attention should be given to the structure of the dispute resolution or arbitral clause within a commercial contract. Optimising the efficiency of these clauses is achieved through the drafting of a multi-tiered arbitral clause.

10

POWER AND NEGOTIATION

Negotiation is about power. It revolves around power. I believe that this is an underlying truth to all negotiations. In an earlier chapter, we discussed the approaches of either being co-operative or competitive or a combination of both. It is reasonably safe to assume – whether any of the counterparties would care to admit it or not – that the varying levels of power between the individuals or organisations involved would be a significant determinant in how they (a particular party/individual) were going to participate in proceedings. Power is an interesting thing as it has significant ramifications regarding how it is used. There are a variety of different types of power that an organisation or an individual may possess. From the organisational perspective, a corporate entity may be powerful due to its market share. Perhaps it is a single point of supply for a proprietary technology and has no competitors. It could be a large buyer. It may be 'best in class.' Perhaps the organisation controls the distribution channels within a marketplace. It may be the leader in R&D and innovation, or it could have financial strength. It might be fully integrated and control the supply chain backwards and forwards.

From the individual perspective, someone can also be powerful from a variety of perspectives. They might possess positional power (i.e. they are someone important), their job or office (title) may convey power onto them. They may be very informed (super important for the negotiator) and possess an insight into matters that other don't have. They may be very educated and have a broad base of knowledge that enables them to 'ad lib' (think on their feet) very quickly. They might be a natural leader, an excellent and persuasive speaker and be very charismatic. They may be capable of influencing

DOI: 10.4324/9781003263722-10

others to their position or point of view. The truth is though, the above points aside, everyone has power. Let me share with you one of my favourite stories about power. Quite a number of years ago, I began teaching at a local university (through Stone Falcon) as a bit of a hobby. On my first day, I drove in and parked. As I got out of my car, I noticed a weather-beaten serious looking man in a high visibility jacket closely inspecting the parked cars. I called over to him and asked him if it was alright to park where I was. He came over, a scowl firmly etched onto his face. I held out my hand and introduced myself, explaining that I was going to be starting to lecture here. He seemed quite taken aback, shaking my hand as if mesmerised. He then looked at my car and informed me that I didn't have a parking sticker. I explained to him that no one had told me about this. He was watching me closely as he explained that it cost £500 per year for the sticker but the parking was still on a 'first come, first serve' basis. I said that I thought that was ridiculous. He looked at me (for the sake of the story, let's call him Dave) and informed me that I was the first lecturer type who hadn't treated him as if he was something that they'd found on the bottom of their shoe. He took a note of my registration and told me to park wherever I wanted – which I did. Sometimes if I was running a little late, I would even park in the visitor's spaces right outside the doors. Well, in the course of things, it transpired that Dave was waging a war single-handed against the academic staff, and making a lot of their lives an absolute misery. Colleagues of mine parked miles away from the campus, trudging in through pouring rain and freezing snow and winds rather than incur a £60 penalty that went to a debt collection agency (as it seemed that no one found the £500 'official sticker' option attractive). So Dave was a powerful person within his domain and yet other people who were perhaps a little self-important failed to recognise this. His power and the power he transferred to me by having carte blanche where I parked made my life far more comfortable and I was never late for meetings or classes. Moral of the story – everyone's got power; get them on your side and you'll be amazed what transpires. At the end of the day, it doesn't have to be artifice. Simply treat people with respect as you yourself would like to be treated. This is true in all things.

In the next chapter, I discuss how various aspects of speech represent a powerful combination of tools for establishing and maintaining control within a negotiation. On the point of influencing others and thus having power, the author feels it more appropriate to discuss the 'Art of Persuasion' in a bit more detail in this chapter rather than the next (although there is an overlap). I am very fond of saying to people when I am training negotiators that there is 'no-reality, only perception.' This may sound like a rather strange statement, but if the reader pauses to consider this, they might see the truth in it. On this basis, it is important for a negotiator to attempt to understand the counterparty's perception of the situation. I always start by asking myself what motivates them. From this question, I try to consider what it is that I think they want, what they are trying to achieve as well as what they don't want and are trying to avoid. A good key to this conundrum is to consider self-interest (discussed earlier) – everyone starts from a position of self-interest. If you can persuade the other parties that what you are proposing is beneficial to them, they might accept your proposition. I believe that there are two keys that are the enablers for effective persuasion. First, understand with clarity that no matter what, the other party will arrive at the table with preconceptions, opinions and beliefs before anything even starts. Second, in order to be persuasive, you have to be very good at communicating your position and be able to work this communication based on your understanding of the counterparty's position and behaviour. Keen observation of this will enable you to make adjustments to your persuasion tactics as the process unfolds. Remember, you can miss an opportunity, literally with the blink of an eye.

So, what becomes clearly evident then is that power is a multifaceted thing, and by making an assessment of the Power Perception Matrix (Figure 10.1) as part of your due diligence process, I would suggest that you can identify where any leverage that you might have may lay as well as anything that you should be concerned about (i.e. where the counterparty might have some advantage).

The way to use Figure 10.1 is to draw three columns on a page. List all the specific sources of power that fall under organisational, individual or both, as they relate to your perspective of the upcoming negotiation. Next, repeat the process as best you can (consult your due diligence information) in the same way for the counterparty. The third step is to look for power interfaces – areas of potential interaction. For example, if we consider Figure 10.1, your

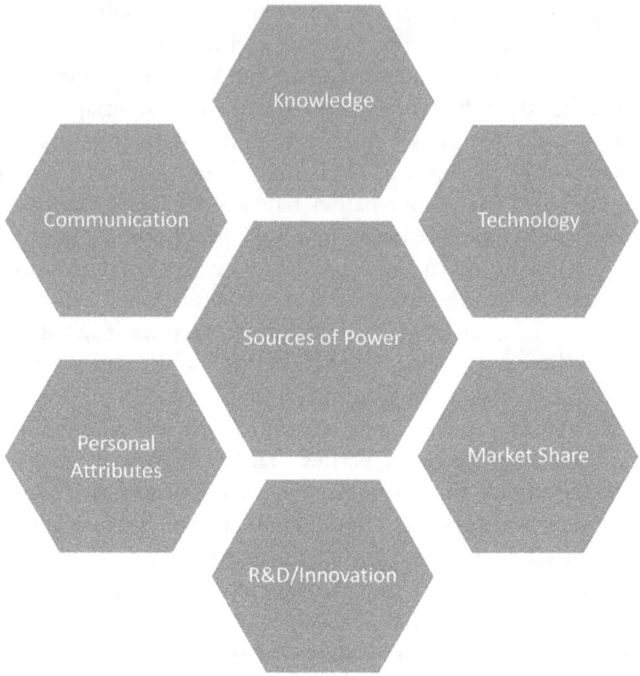

Figure 10.1 The Power Perception Matrix.

organisation has the biggest market share, but the counterparty has unique, cutting-edge technology and are fantastic at R&D – there is a power interface here between the parties. What I mean by a power interface is that this is an area where two different sources of power meet. If the purpose of the negotiation, for example, is to create a joint venture, then this interface represents a synergistic opportunity for both parties. The power interface will therefore be a central aspect of consideration by everyone prior to commencement of the negotiation.

Silver Bullet: Negotiation strategies and tactics revolve around power. How it is used represents a significant impact on the final outcome of the negotiation process as well as often defining important aspects of longer-term relationships.

11

ESTABLISHING AND MAINTAINING CONTROL

Silver Bullet: Before you can establish any control over the negotiation proceedings, you must be in control of yourself.

Whilst the Silver Bullet above may sound rather zen-like, I believe that it is nonetheless a fundamental truth when it comes to commercial negotiations. Although modern living has dulled and suppressed many of our instincts, humans still possess a residual ability to inherently distil information from the behaviour of others. Elite-level negotiators have honed these abilities to be as sharp as possible. In an earlier chapter, we discussed body language and the spoken word. It is a wide and deep subject matter area and the author believes it is probable that many more secrets are yet to be unlocked. To return to the negotiation table, the first thing that I believe the negotiator must do is be in complete control of their emotions. Humans can smell fear. Individuals will see worry, panic or uncertainty written on your face or revealed in your voice or expressed by your body language. Your emotions will betray you at the table. You must be calm and show an unreadable expression. If you remain silent and have a good poker face, you are immediately harnessing an advantage. Why? Your stance on a matter is only revealed when you speak, when you express your opinion. One of the biggest giveaways in my experience is the slight nodding people engage in when listening to something they agree with; to a receptive counterparty, they will know that you approve. You don't want them to know that you approve. You want them to know as little as possible until such time as you are willing to commit an opinion, be it positive or negative. Silence, coupled with an unreadable expression and a perfectly still

DOI: 10.4324/9781003263722-11

body, is a powerful weapon that keeps the counterparty unsure of what your position actually is. An interesting aspect of this is that sometimes, individuals feel that they have to say more to 'fill in' the silences. I can remember many a time where someone has inadvertently given away an important fact through excess verbiage.

There is no room for subjectivity in commercial negotiations. The negotiator must be coldly objective, deal in the currency of facts and nothing else. Around the table, subjectivity and emotive responses must be completely suppressed. An elite-level negotiator will be able to take everything that I have said in this chapter and use it in a 'mirror image' strategy. Their control is such that they will deliberately give away signals, such as the slight nodding or having a particular expression as a powerful form of misdirection. They will create a persona, an image that is carefully crafted so that the counterparty believes that they have your measure. If this is done successfully, they can operate with relative impunity from behind this façade, as simply, people see what they want to see.

It is important that should the negotiator find themselves in a bad situation (i.e. the negotiation is rapidly spinning off-track, important elements and concessions have not been realised, the disadvantage of their relative position is magnifying by the minute), then they should have the mental resilience to continue to operate as above. It is important to understand that whatever the current situation may be, there is likely going to be an opportunity to rest and regroup sooner or later (if not, make one; suggest a break). In every situation, opportunities present themselves. It's just being ready to grasp them. I like to think of mental resilience, toughness and endurance collectively as Psychic Armour and having the ability to adapt and morph with the situation as Psychic Camouflage.

Silver Bullet: The negotiator who seems impervious to worry or stress, maintains control regardless of the situation within which they find themselves around the negotiation table and who are capable of adaptation and 'flow' to harness emergent opportunities and advantages have developed Psychic Armour and possess Psychic Camouflage.

So far in this chapter, we have discussed control from the personal perspective (i.e. having control over yourself). In an earlier chapter, we discussed at length control that could be exercised over the physical location of the negotiation (lighting, Wi-Fi, comfort etc.). The third dimension, of course, is possessing or creating some modicum of control over the proceedings themselves. Whilst the easiest and most recognisable element of this is to have an established agenda with issues and points to be worked through logically, this does not necessarily equate with establishing control over the behaviour of the counterparties. You might have an agenda, but so might they. If this is the case, they are likely to diverge from one another (hence the negotiation).

One of the key elements to master in order to gain control is The Art of Questioning. The author believes that there are four components to mastering this 'Art':

1 **Psychological understanding of people** – knowing how people think and why they think in a particular manner (consider elements such as education, nationality/culture, gender, behavioural norms and values, degree of experience as a negotiator [consider earlier comments regarding misdirection]).
2 **Physiological understanding of people** – knowing the meaning of postures/body language, appearance and other non-verbal clues. Understanding verbal clues: tone, inflection, volume and so forth.
3 **Understanding that 1 and 2 above are the two halves of human behaviour** – we are all the sum product of our experiences.
4 **Practice** – being able to harness the Art of Questioning does not come naturally. It takes practice – a lot of it.

In my opinion, questions fall into two broad categories: they are either 'open' questions or 'closed' questions. It is important to understand that there is a lot going on psychologically when one person is questioning another. Response will be influenced/impacted upon by the physical environment as well as how comfortable and relaxed an individual may feel and whether or not they are in a co-operative mood (e.g. consider the contrast with being interrogated in a police cell, to having an easy conversation in a smart restaurant). The author has learned from long experience that how you ask questions will largely determine the amount of information given in the response. People react to closed questions by focusing on the question itself – they don't generally supply anything more in their answer except the bare requirements – whilst open questions tend to encourage the other party to talk freely, often supplying a wealth of information.

An example of closed questioning:

Q: 'Are you married?' A: 'Yes I am.'
Q: 'How long have you been married?' A: 'Six years.'
Q: 'Do you have any children?' A: 'Yes.'
Q: 'How many?' A: 'Two.'
Q: 'Girls or boys?' A: 'One of each.'

As can be seen by this line of questioning, utilising closed questions tend to reveal information incrementally, especially within the context of the parties being unfamiliar with one another. The process becomes time-consuming and, in my opinion, frustrating. Contrast this with the example below of asking open questions:

Q: 'I see by your wedding band that you are married. Can you tell me about your family?'

A: 'Of course. My husband is called Robert – we all call him Bob – he's an architect. We have been married for six years and had our honeymoon in the Caribbean, as Bob and I are keen scuba divers. We have two children, a boy called Frederick and a girl called Louise. Frederick is the oldest, he is hoping to go to university and study law in a few years – he's at school at the moment. Louise is very interested in marine biology.'

If the reader considers the difference in response to the open as opposed to the closed question, it should become immediately evident what can be achieved through utilising the correct application. Often, open questions contain a primer – a bit of stage setting or a lead-in statement. In the example above, it is easy to imagine that the parties are relaxed and comfortable, the questioner uses the primer 'I see by your wedding band that you are married.' The actual question then flows seamlessly from this statement. People like to talk about themselves and (even if subconsciously) are flattered by someone showing an interest in them. Because they reveal so much more information, open questions can sometimes be used as a means of discovery. The lead-in statement can be a bluff, where you are giving the impression that you know something. If the lead-in statement and question are put the right way, the information you were fishing for can often be revealed and a fact or issue confirmed – perhaps unknowingly by the other party.

For example:

Q: 'The writing is on the wall for the Hydrocarbon Industry – alternative energy sources such as LNG and wind power are looking like they're going to dominate. What's your view on this?'

A: 'We agree that with marginal diminishing offshore assets, it will become necessary to diversify into alternative energy markets, but we are more interested in wind power generation as it is a much cheaper investment strategy than LNG and is better suited to our local environment.'

In the example above (taken from an actual conversation), the intent was to gauge the other party's interest in LNG, as they were considered a potential competitive threat if they were evaluating entering into this market. Note how the true intention (LNG) was rolled up into other information so as to mask our particular focus/interest.

Questions can also be either explicit: 'Who is going to be the project manager?' Or they may be implicit: 'Perhaps we could discuss this further tomorrow?' The reader will notice that the major difference between the two types of questions is that explicit questions tend to be factual, that is, there is a definite answer that is known, whilst implicit questions tend to be suggested or implied, that is, the answer is not asked for definitively.

All of the above have their place in commercial negotiations, as different questions and types of questions have different purposes (see below). An elite-level negotiator will ensure that their questioning technique is blended, that is, a mixture in order to maximise information gain. In my opinion, effective questioning, coupled with superior communication skills, is a very effective way of controlling both the process and the agenda.

The different purposes of questions:

- To discover information
- Confirmation of facts
- Summing up facts

- To develop relationships
- To solve problems
- To reveal new direction/options
- Assessment of progress (i.e. achievement of milestones)
- Assessment of other party's understanding and grasp of information/issues relative to the negotiation

SPEECH – YOUR MOST POWERFUL WEAPON FOR CONTROL

Experience has taught me that within the negotiation environment, speech is a multifaceted tool utilised in a plethora of different ways. I believe that it is the greatest source of power around the negotiation table if you know how to use it. The starting point is often the seeking of common ground with the counterparty – attempting to establish things that you have in common, interests that you might share. In establishing this rapport, consider the value of the previous section: knowing how to ask the right questions. Speech can be phrased such as to be persuasive: to bring the counterparty around to your way of thinking, to agree with you. Sometimes, when there is a significant power imbalance (read chapter relating to power), the pattern of speech may be controlling. Dominance can often be achieved through controlling speech, especially if there is a power imbalance in your favour. Dominance walks hand in hand with manipulation; one of the most common examples of this is utilising someone's name. Someone once told me that if you knew a person's name, you automatically had some power or leverage immediately as opposed to talking to them and not knowing it. Consider how your attention is immediately focused when someone uses your name when addressing you. One of the first things that happens subconsciously is that you feel more valued, more accepted. This therefore makes you more amenable to listening to what someone has to say to you. I believe that it is not only politeness (which is always a good way to start off), but it demonstrates to others that you have made an effort to engage with them.

Other very powerful aspects of what can be achieved with speech are visualisation and analogy. The right words or story enable others to picture what you are saying – they can see it in their minds or they are curious whilst listening to an analogy – mentally searching for the connection, attempting to guess where a particular story is leading. They are focused and engaged. A further dimension to this form of manipulation is that of substitution – choosing terms that will create a desired image or impression in the minds of those listening. You could speak graphically or bluntly sparing no one's feelings, whilst you could also choose to use euphemism to describe something unpleasant in a pleasant way. I view this as the two sides to the verbal coin, considering direct, graphic speech as hard and euphemism as soft. By creating an impression or image in the minds of the counterparty, you are utilising manipulation in a very subtle form. Experience will enable you to develop the perfect blending of hard and soft speech to gain control of a situation, but it will take much practice!

Another aspect to the power of speech within a negotiation context is the use of repetition. If the reader considers the conversation above, then repetition can be added to your narrative. If used correctly, repetition can be a strong influencer. If you have ever had the (unfortunate) experience of listening to a high-pressure salesman, you will note that key factors and benefits are frequently repeated. This is utilised to focus your attention on the positives and distract you away from other possibly less desirable features. Whilst not so crass or so obvious, this is exactly how to use repetition within the negotiation setting: reiterate the positives, downplay the negatives.

One of the oldest (yet still very effective) forms of manipulation through speech is that of flattery. Whether we like it or not, we all have egos and having them stroked by strangers, colleagues or generally by anyone else always has a positive subconscious effect upon the recipient. Flattery can take many forms. It might appeal to the intellect, make reference to an individual's achievements and position, comment on their looks or appearance, but perhaps most importantly, flattery can be used as a great amplifier when combined with repetition. The danger of course is that you come across as insincere, which will nullify (probably completely, if not to a large extent) your credibility. Around the negotiation table, credibility is hard currency.

The power of suggestion should never be discounted. In the hands of an elite-level negotiator who is able to utilise all of the aspects of speech discussed thus far into a coherent strategy, a direct suggestion made within this context often establishes control. If you suggest that something should be so or that those around the table should consider 'x' and individuals comply, then you have control. Marketing is all about suggestion, in many subtle ways, not just by the obvious direct approach. Much of what we have discussed in this section can be seen in modern advertising: the tone and manner of speech, the imagery conveyed, the suggestion planted. Consider many music videos or adverts that suggest a lifestyle. The idea is to get the consumer to subscribe, to buy into the fantasy, and that by association, you can be like the people in the advert, or walk down that beach, or drink in that bar and so forth. I'm sure the reader sees where I'm going with this. Suggestion can also be brought about through innuendo – the implied thing – such as taking someone into your confidence and informing them of something that you know and are sharing with them, thus creating the co-conspirator syndrome, implicating them through your gesture of trust and, in turn, binding them to it. In the author's opinion, suggestion is most effective if it is a fluid communication strategy: constantly evolving with the situation, constantly flowing. Putting everything together should maximise your ability to speak and present around the negotiation table – to be in control. The Silver Bullet below suggests ten important tips of presentation that I believe will make a significant difference to anyone not utilising them all.

Silver Bullet: Some key tips on presentation skills:

1. **Know what you're talking about**
2. **Be confident; an audience can smell fear**
3. **Engage with your audience**
4. **Vary the cadence/tone/emphasis of your voice**
5. **Maintain eye contact with all of your audience, don't just stare at a fixed spot**
6. **Know your audience, pitch at the right level**
7. **Bring your audience with you, the buy in factor**
8. **Be entertaining**
9. **Don't (in the majority of cases) take yourself too seriously**
10. **Don't be aggressive and hostile towards your audience**

12

DECEPTION, MISDIRECTION, LYING AND HALF-TRUTHS

All human interaction is very complex, and this is especially so around the negotiation table where parties are often engaged in a 'psychological gladiatorial' contest: circling around one another cautiously, probing, looking for a weakness/opportunity, feinting and retracting, striking and defending, it's all there. The weapons though, as discussed throughout this book, are knowledge, words and facts. The awareness and ability to assimilate knowledge quickly provides the advantage or being the possessor of valuable knowledge unknown to the counterparty – deception and misdirection the armour to confuse, enabled by lying and half-truths.

Several times throughout this book, I have mentioned the concept of self-interest and the fact that if we are honest with ourselves, we subconsciously want to know how we will benefit from a situation – what's in it for us. The author believes that quite often, the way in which people seek to leverage this self-interest falls within the ambit of this chapter's title. When you meet someone for the first time and they exchange information with you about themselves, I'm willing to bet that there's either a bit of poetic license in terms of what they tell you (i.e. making themselves out to be a little better than they actually are) or even complete fabrication (a polite way of saying lying). I suspect that the most common approach is to tell half-truths; mix in a bit of truth with a bit of fiction, this gives you plausibility. Plausibility is very important within the negotiation context. If you are plausible, it becomes easy to manipulate the perception of the other parties as they will see and hear what they want to, and if you fit these preconceptions, little or no further attention is given to your credibility – attention is focussed on what you are saying.

DOI: 10.4324/9781003263722-12

Deception takes many forms, and regrettably, the author believes that it is all too common within human endeavours and interactions. As a commercial negotiator, you must be aware of the issues discussed above and be as prepared as possible. Understand that some things can be prepared for (i.e. when dealing with tangible facts), whilst the intangible elements of the process can never be fully prepared for, as it is impossible to have perfect knowledge of some future state and to really know what someone else is thinking. Deception also may be deliberate – part of the strategy or it may be unintended (misconception/misunderstanding/miscommunication). I believe that the most dangerous form of deception (as it is very difficult to deal with) is opportunistic deception. This occurs when some advantage has been inadvertently given away, perhaps by a slip of the tongue, perhaps by someone sharing a document that they shouldn't have and the counterparty realising that they have just been given a gift to utilise to their advantage. A good way to be prepared for this happening is to be able to exercise the self-control discussed earlier: to remain impassive, to say nothing, to hold your face and body still. This, in itself, may actually prevent the counterparty from realising that a mistake has been made. Silence and self-control should be thought of as a counter-deception, a deception on your part that seeks to nullify any deceptive strategies that could arise from the counterparty's inadvertent advantage by acting as if no advantage had been given away.

Silver Bullet: All forms of deception can be very damaging, if discovered. When practicing deception, the aim and intent should be for it never to come to light. In the event that it is discovered, the deceiver should have a strategy of plausible deniability – providing disclosure as to why, further diluting the truth by mixing in more half-truths and attempting to limit the damage done.

Silver Bullet: The best defence against discovery of deception is the Double O Strategy, a strategy of Opaqueness and Obfuscation. Utilise your knowledge of the person to whom you are lying. Create the right impression. The way you are dressed, your body language and your manner of speech must all be matched to the context at hand.

Deception is made possible through lying. When individuals lie, regardless of the context, they are deceiving someone else. Lying is a complex thing. It can represent a moral dilemma (i.e. lying to protect someone else's feelings or to protect them from something). Lying to cheat someone in some manner or to gain an advantage over them, there appears to be a 'lying continuum' as to how serious a lie may or may not be. But the problem with this is that it is once more down to perception. It is easy to fool ourselves with rationality as to why we lied about something. I think that there are two kinds of people in the world: liars and those that lie. It is perhaps an uncomfortable truth that we lie, but people do and that's the truth! The author is of the opinion that the most common form of lying (mentioned at the start of the chapter) is lying to impress. What I have always found particularly interesting is that to me, it seems that men do this much more than women, often when a man is attempting to impress a woman that they have just met! In my experience, I have found that there is no significant difference between men and women when it comes to lying. It's just that they tend to have different reasons for doing so. As discussed above, men will often lie to impress, whereas I have found that the most common reason why woman generally lie is to try to avoid hurting people's feelings (outwith a commercial context).

What has always deeply amused the author is that to recognise that lying is a very common human trait, we have to be honest. Attitudes towards lying are very interesting as it depends upon with whom you speak to. Some people believe that dishonesty is a crime or a sin and one should never tell lies under any circumstances. Others believe in 'white lies,' small lies that can protect others. Some people (and I've known a few of these within the commercial world) think that lying is a great tool for achieving success and advancement, whilst others believe that lying is justified within certain situations. Nevertheless, lying is a skill and not everyone is good at it. Truth is absolutely tied to perception. It is a simple truth in itself that for every situation, there are always a number of truths – the truth according to a particular party, the truth according to the other (or another) party and the truth itself. Everyone has their own version of what is true or not, and this is often representative of a central problem/issue for the commercial negotiation process, attempting to discern what is actually true and what is not.

Silver Bullet: The Essence of Lying is to project honesty without having any sense of guilt and therefore to believe the lie yourself when using it, but not confusing it with the truth. A conscience only bothers you if you have one – there are many out there who are not worried about sleeping at night. You may easily encounter such an individual around the negotiation table. Always be on your guard as much as possible for this eventuality.

I believe that there is a process to deliberate deception or misdirection through what is said or communicated to the counterparties (not all communication is verbal). You start with something that is absolutely true – this is your anchor or starting point. The next information you utilise is diluted truth – you build on your anchor point and the additional information that you give has some further truth to it – but is diluted by falsehood. This sets you up for telling a lie, building on the plausibility of the story that you have told so far. The intention is that the combination of whole truth, half-truth and lie will all represent stages of progress towards your target, whatever it may be. Words can be used to create an image, a representation. Often, if people choose their words very carefully – they are not lying at all – they are simply allowing your brain to draw erroneous conclusions.

The author remembers a guy who worked offshore in Aberdeen. He was a labourer (roustabout) on the rigs and drove an ancient BMW that was a complete wreck. I happened to bump into him in a bar in Cape Town one night and was absolutely amused to hear him telling an attentive young lady that 'he worked offshore in the Oil Industry in Aberdeen and drove a BMW.' She was quite enthralled with his obvious success/wealth and status. He hadn't told a word of a lie! Around the negotiation table, allowing others to think something that you actually haven't said is a very powerful form of misdirection. The other parties are actually misdirecting themselves!

Generally, I think that most of us lacking any specialised training are not too accurate at telling whether someone is lying to us. As there are two sides to every coin, a person in reality could be right half the time in detecting an untruth told to them; but this is not quite so straightforward, as the issue tends to be clouded by a variety of other psychological factors and reasons. For example, sometimes you simply want to believe what you are being told and this is closely coupled to 'hearing what you want to hear' – you have a belief in someone or something and do not want this tarnished or altered in your mind/perception. Perhaps this is uncomfortable and you do not want to deviate from your position or held beliefs. Another factor here is that human nature makes some of us too trusting and some of us too suspicious. So, if someone is lying to us, we believe it (assuming we're the too trusting type), whilst if someone is telling the truth, we disbelieve it (being too suspicious). Obviously, both of these can be counterproductive and work against us. To further cloud this issue, the author has met a fair share of individuals who claim that they 'know' when someone is lying to them through the use of their 'intuition'. I don't mean to sound cynical, but I've seen people's intuition lead them off in the wrong direction spectacularly all the while being convinced that they're on the money (another example of believing what we want to believe). DON'T rely on intuition within a negotiation context – whatever you do!

There are also a lot of myths about how to tell if someone is lying to you. Two of my favourites are the eye contact and movement legends. Whilst there is a modicum of truth that if someone is lying, they may find it difficult to look you in the eyes (consider my earlier statement about a conscience only bothering you if you have one) – if they feel guilty or uncomfortable about lying to you – but if they don't, then this is irrelevant. It is relatively easy (in the author's opinion) to make a conscious effort to engage in steady eye contact and not tell the truth or the whole truth. The other popular one is that if someone is excessively fidgeting, then they are being untruthful or deceitful in what they are telling you. What if they are just extremely nervous and/or uncomfortable? This theory will then lead you off on a useless tangent. The idea of body language being a good sign or readability only holds water in as far as the individual concerned. For example, I will often sit around the negotiation table with my arms folded across my chest. Body language gurus will tell you that this is defensive and that I am 'putting up a barrier' and that I am not comfortable. I will tell you this is utter rubbish. I sit this way as I find it very comfortable, especially when listening and mentally evaluating what is being said. Furthermore, an elite-level negotiator can mask all of these things to deliberately allow other parties to draw erroneous conclusions (mentioned earlier). So, it would be very easy for me to sit this way to make the counterparty think that I'm on edge, and therefore lead them off in a wild speculation as to why I'm obviously uncomfortable and nervous. This will distract them from their focus. Negotiators need to be focused – at all times.

Sometimes, the *way* or the *manner* in which someone is talking can reveal that they are being untruthful. Certain habits or patterns of speech tend to be indicative of mistruths and an observant, listening individual can home in on these. Sometimes, a person has a lot to say. They use a lot of words; yet if you listen to them, they don't actually say anything, especially if asked a direct question. This circumlocution (excessive verbiage) and/or evasion are normally clear signs of mistruth. Another giveaway has always been very interesting to me as it represents the exact opposite end of the speech spectrum. Yet, either is used interchangeably, giving very short answers to questions or utilising very broad descriptors that, as mentioned above, don't say very much. They lack any real, significant detail.

Speech is also used for mental misdirection – bending or distorting facts that the speaker knows will cause confusion (also consider half-truths, discussed above). On occasion, when someone is spinning a story, the lack of pronoun usage and vague generalisations are a dead giveaway. It is almost as if the liar wants to ensure that they are telling the truth about their non-involvement, so avoid using words like 'me,' 'I' or, in the case of being uncertain about who was actually involved in something, avoiding usage of 'he,' 'she.' The human mind is a strange thing!

Perhaps the indication of mistruth that we are all the most familiar with is when someone prefaces a tale with statements like 'I promise you this is really true' or 'You're never going to believe this.' Generally speaking, such pronouncements lead us to doubt the veracity of the story to follow.

The last speech mannerism that I believe is a sign of untruth (as mentioned above) is the *way* that an individual is speaking – the cadence (the speed of their speech and the use of pauses). Both these habits will generally indicate to me that a person is unsure of themselves or are trying to think and talk their way out of something by trying to sound plausible (discussed earlier).

All of these indicators – speech, facial expression, body language and so forth – most definitely carry subliminal information, yet the negotiator must ensure that they are not being deliberately misled or deceived into believing something that is the actual intention of the counterparty (i.e. misdirection). All these things must be taken collectively – a holistic approach is needed. Those who understand the integrated nature of human signs of untruth are far likely able to spot it, understand it and deal with it.

Silver Bullet: Lying is an integrated activity with many elements. Do not focus on one particular thing. Watch for and consider all the signs emanating from an individual across the table. The signs will always be there in some form. It's just knowing what to watch for.

13

STRATEGIES AND TACTICS OF NEGOTIATION

Silver Bullet: Strategies are the blueprint, the map. Tactics are the means of operational delivery of implementing the strategy. Strategy should always be the big picture with a longer-term focus. Tactics however are the 'fighting in the trenches,' dealing with what is in front of you now.

When considering the planning, execution and implementation of a negotiation strategy, the singular key thing that the negotiator must always acknowledge is that they are operating within the domain of uncertainty. In the first instance, the level of uncertainty can most definitely be mitigated or reduced to a degree by careful and thorough planning and preparation. The problem though is that negotiations are dynamic processes and the mode of uncertainty may shift at any given moment, so it is better to consider it a constant. The negotiator should remember that uncertainty in itself is a double-edged sword; it may present threats, but it can also provide opportunities. When I am attempting to quantify uncertainty prior to a negotiation (as much as I can), I tend to prepare myself by identifying the sources of where uncertainty might arise. First, the most obvious one is the agenda of the counterparties. You can never be absolutely certain what their objectives and goals might be. Second is attempting to assess what is true or false (see discussion in previous chapter). Third is looking/listening for ambiguity in either speech or documentation. This is very dangerous, particularly within the drafting of a contract, and must be removed. Fourth, with shifts in the environment, there is always the possibility of the impact of random events. Following are two quick examples on this point. I once negotiated a deal and

DOI: 10.4324/9781003263722-13

when concluded, it was to the complete satisfaction of everyone concerned. There were no grey areas and everything had been discussed and agreed in detail. The date of actual signing was deferred as the contract was going to be drafted by the counterparty's legal department and the principal of the counterparty was going on two weeks leave. During this time, the principal was offered an early retirement package that he couldn't say no to. He completed a thorough handover with his successor and left the organisation. In due course, I found myself back at the table to sign the deal. The new guy disagreed with the financials and investment requirements and wanted to renegotiate. The whole thing fell apart with startling rapidity as parties became entrenched in their perspective. It was felt by my side that this was nonsense and, in a way, a betrayal. We walked away and secured a similar deal with another party that proved equally beneficial to us. What this particular story illustrates as well as sudden change – is the importance of reaching the exit point and leaving.

The other example is pretty similar, except that the principal of the counterparty sadly fell into sudden ill health and passed away from a heart attack before the contract had been formally signed. Once more, replacements wanted to be the 'new broom' sweeping clean, wanting to renegotiate the entire deal with far more unfavourable terms to us. We reached that exit point and we walked from the table. We never came back. I believe that these two stories serve to illustrate the final (and perhaps) most important source of uncertainty within a commercial negotiation – the outcome.

A key element to both the strategy and any tactics employed is when and to what degree to make any disclosures. The timing of disclosures is not only of critical importance, but can have a magnitude of effect on the process not dissimilar to that of a tsunami. When making the disclosure choice, the author always considers what's at stake. A disclosure may weaken your position, but this may be in the immediate or short term and may have longer-term benefits. I always consider the comparison between winning or losing the battle against winning or losing the war. Sometimes, for the longer-term benefit, it is necessary or sensible to make a short-term sacrifice. The negotiator must always weigh this up. It's important in the extreme. It must also be remembered that the above aside, sometimes non-disclosure could equate to deception and this might make the contract voidable. This misrepresentation could also potentially result in litigation and could be considered/construed as fraud. Statements made by parties in the course of a commercial negotiation are not considered as facts legally, unless they are absolutely true and can prove to be so (irrefutable). Needless to say, it is always prudent to be cautious in what is said around the table.

An important preparation that every negotiator must make is to build in elements of movement in both their overarching strategy and their tactical implementation. There is no place for rigidity and intractability if it is nothing more than either stupidity or stubbornness. It is of vital importance that the concept of trade-off processes exists within your plans.

Silver Bullet: Trade-off decision-making and processes are an essential element to a successful negotiation strategy and tactical implementation. There is no place for rigidity or inflexibility if you want a positive result.

In order to include this element, it is first necessary for those involved to have as much clarity as possible in the identification and definition of the objectives and criteria to be met (i.e. the purpose of the negotiation). These objectives and criteria must be ranked according to importance and prioritised accordingly. During this process, the negotiator/negotiation team should conduct a review of the objectives and criteria and make an honest assessment if the 'scope' (what is wanted to be achieved) is streamlined. Failure to do this often leads to wasted time as the negotiation process gets side-tracked or goes off on a tangent focused on peripheral issues rather than precision at the core. Once the negotiator/negotiation team is satisfied with these points and issues, they must then identify options and alternative outcomes. Those involved should always have a fall-back point that is acceptable prior to the exit point (the point of no return – where it's over and cannot/will not be salvaged or resurrected). There are a number of ways that the fall-back position can be evaluated against the negotiation strategy. The starting point for me has always been to achieve alignment between issues and objectives and the level of uncertainty surrounding them. For me, this gives an estimation of predictability and certainty as to the likelihood of success and realistic accomplishment of them. As mentioned earlier in the book, there is nearly always a value differential between different items associated with the negotiation from the perspective of the counterparties. I like to think of these things as the 'burnables'; things that to me are expendable and can be burnt off in the course of the negotiation as long as a 'counter gain' is made, that is, the other party will also have burnables. This is a very effective form of 'horse trading' in moving a negotiation forward as issues are settled through *quid pro quo*. Sometimes though, it might not be immediately apparent that something is tradable or expendable to you or to the counterparty. This is why a positive dialogue and an active exploration of issues around the table can sometimes (and often does) result in an improved deal for everyone, even if it wasn't apparent at first. As negotiation is such a fluid, uncertain process, it is always important to be aware of or create alternatives and options. As I stated earlier, there is no place for rigidity or intractability around the negotiation table if you want results.

Silver Bullet: It is always of paramount importance to be aware of or create alternative courses of actions and different options as the situation unfolds.

When I have identified and assessed viable options, I always rank the potential alternatives. I examine, consider and assess these alternatives from a scenario perspective and question how they align with the different potential outcomes that could materialise, that is, optimistic, pessimistic or most probable.

The author believes that there are always a number of different tactics or approaches that can be taken within a negotiation scenario and would like to share some of what I believe to be the most efficient and effective strategies and tactics that I have acquired over the years with you, the reader. Remember that all these must be considered from a duality perspective, either from the point of view that you are the individual harnessing these methods or that you are facing them. There is no '100% guarantee of success' in anything that happens around the table, but I hope that these strategies and tactics will prove useful and add value.

THE 'SILENT MAN'

When a negotiation is about to take place, the counterparties engage within the ritual of either acknowledging a known associate or acquaintance and ensuring that everyone is introduced to one another. What this is actually doing is subconsciously giving everyone a chance to size up one another, to formulate their first impressions and consider how they think particular individuals will act and what this might mean for the negotiation to come. We all try to assess and gauge the interactions that are going to occur. What we are doing is attempting, in fact, to mitigate uncertainty, even at a subconscious level. This is very important, for to 'be in the zone' or 'be on your game' you want to feel that you have a modicum of control (discussed earlier). It is all a question of being balanced,' being composed and ready for the task and challenges that lies ahead.

The issue of being balanced is probably the singular most important preparation for the commercial negotiator. It's taking a mental inventory of oneself: checking off plans, going over information, attempting to foresee any last-minute problems. This process is taking place even as the aforementioned sizing up is occurring; a part of the negotiator's mind is busy making assessments and judgements, evaluating new information as it is presented. The greatest initial advantage that one can achieve is to upset this balance of the counterparties by altering something unexpectedly or introducing an unknown factor.

Silver Bullet: In negotiations of any form, mental balance is imperative to achieve anything. In the author's opinion, all negotiation strategies and tactics are designed to unbalance the counterparty in some way as this decreases their operational efficiency and gains some form of advantage or serves some purpose.

This is where the 'Silent Man' strategy comes into play. There are a number of variations on this that I have used over the years. The first of these is to either speak very little (only enough to be polite) or don't speak at all. As discussed earlier, utilising silence, coupled with an impassive face and body language, make you unreadable. No one knows what your position is until you articulate it, and if you are saying nothing, it becomes a distraction to the counterparty, as they devote mental energy into trying to figure you out asking themselves numerous questions as to you and your role.

A stronger version of this is to have someone else present who is unknown to the parties about to commence the negotiation proceedings. You observe the formalities and introduce the individual in question, BUT don't explain who they are or why they are present.

When I have utilised this approach and someone has enquired as to who the stranger may be/what role do they have, I often like to be deliberately vague and use phrases like 'John is here to observe.' John will take no part in the proceedings but might from time to time make some facial expressions and jot down some notes. This has a great unbalancing effect as curiosity equates to uncertainty. Do not believe for a moment that a bit of acting doesn't go a long way!

THE THIRD PERSON

A further refinement on the previous two is to take it a step further – have someone new appear at the last moment. Introduce them quickly and begin proceedings. Ideally, place them sitting behind you against the wall if the room layout allows or can be designed to accommodate this or, if not, alongside you at the table. The key to causing the unbalance here or confusion is to appear to be quite deferential to this newcomer. Again, they utilise silence – body and facial expression (and lack thereof). I remember working for a guy who was one very switched-on operator when it came to negotiating. He once got his PA to take the janitor into town to be groomed and bought him a nice suit and shoes – having asked him to 'do him a small favour.' We were all quite bemused, but to cut a long story short – the janitor (let's call him Fred) was told (and he looked completely different with a haircut/neatly trimmed beard and suit on) to knock softy on the door of the boardroom, having waited for the negotiation to have started for five or so minutes. Fred was briefed to walk in and not be surprised when the MD made a big fuss of him, thanking him for attending and to take a seat close behind the MD. He was told to lean forward periodically and say something softly in the MD's ear. He asked what he should say and was told 'anything.' I personally wondered whether Fred would be up to this, but he performed admirably. His appearance and especially the deference he received from the MD sowed considerable confusion in the ranks of the counterparties, to put it mildly. Everyone knew that the MD was the owner of the business and were perplexed as to who Fred was. Though clearly someone very important, perhaps a silent partner or a major investor, I could literally see these thoughts going through the minds of the guys on the other side of the table. Every time Fred leaned over and spoke softly in the MD's ear (to which the MD would imperceptibly nod whilst keeping his expression blank and his eyes forward, as if what was being said was of tremendous significance), the counterparty was very distracted. After the negotiation, which proved very successful for us, I got a moment with Fred and wanted to know what he'd said when he'd leant over. He laughed and said that he was quite nervous (though credit to him he didn't show it) as to what to say, so decided to comment on the weather. He'd said things like 'the sky is blue' or 'do you see those clouds moving towards us' and 'I think it might rain later on.' This strategy had worked so well that I have always utilised this in my repertoire to this day. Believe it or not, it is incredibly powerful!

THE 'SPECIALIST TEAM APPROACH'

Many years ago, the author encountered a style of negotiation that involved having a large negotiation team containing specialists in every possible aspect related to the negotiation at hand. So the team would contain, for instance, the finance, engineering and legal specialists who could address any specific detail relating to their subject matter expertise. If executed correctly, it is a powerful and effective strategy and set of tactics. It revolves around preparation and being knowledgeable about the issues at hand as well as who the counterparty is. There is a thorough approach to the due diligence process. As mentioned, the concept of operating in this manner is to ensure that the team is prepared and capable of addressing questions of any kind that might arise. In my experience, the team leader sits in the central position at the table opposite their counterpart. They do most of the talking on behalf of the team, but will nominate a colleague, who, for instance, will be a finance specialist, to address any questions of a financial nature. We would often find three of us sitting across from a team of eight, each having a functional expertise, having 'all bases covered' so to speak. The strength in this approach is that you are unlikely to get caught out by narrow, specialist questions and therefore have the capability to deal with practically anything that might arise. Also, you might intimidate the smaller opposition team, making them nervous as to whether or not they are sufficiently prepared and can handle questions from your specialists.

The downside to this approach can be the cost and time and the logistics involved of getting a large team somewhere else in the world. For this approach to work, the key is discipline and effective team leadership. There has to be a conductor for the orchestra, a ring master for the circus (although some negotiations turn exactly into a form of circus – hopefully it's not the case!). If discipline is lacking, then decision-making may become ponderous and turgid and you might present a disunited front to the counterparty.

THE WATER STRATEGY

A long time ago, I was going to be involved in what proved to be a very tough negotiation. It wasn't friendly, it was time pressured and it involved some complex matters and high stakes. Some time prior to the commencement date, I remember sitting and thinking about how I was going to approach this. I felt that I needed something to give me an edge, a strategy unlike anything I'd ever utilised or improvised ('ad-libbing' is a vital skill for the negotiator). I went to the beach to watch the sea as this had always made me relax and become introspective and thoughtful. It was a beautiful day with a trail of molten gold drizzling over the sea from the reflection of the sun. The last time I'd been down on the beach had been a few days previously during a mighty storm; that's when it struck me – how powerful water was, yet capable of changing so much. I sat down on a rock and began to think about the nature of the sea and water and the numerous parallels I could envision with a negotiation strategy – so was born what became, to me, 'The Water Strategy.' This is the very first time I've ever revealed this story or explained its origin. I always said I would when I wrote my book on commercial negotiation.

If we consider some of the earlier conversations in the book, something that I have been quite repetitive about is the need to be patient, in control and not reveal anything about your thoughts or position on matters. These, to me, are the elements of silence and stillness (two of the fundamental properties of water): to be seen, but not to be heard and to be still and give nothing away through posture or body language. Beneath the surface, there is always movement and a restless abundance of energy. The currents run deep, but they run with direction and purpose. So, this must be the outward face you present to those around the table. Internally, though, your mind must be focussed and active. You are listening, you are assessing and you are planning moves and countermoves, assessing options and identifying alternatives. What comes to the surface should be only that which you want seen, even if it is an illusion. The Japanese have a term *Suigetsu* ('Moonlight on the Water'); this principle generally refers to the idea that you can see something, but it is not real. It is an illusion that is being reflected. This is also part of the 'Art of the Negotiator,' as mentioned throughout: the idea of 'projecting' facial expression and/or body language deliberately, allowing the counterparty to see something right in front of them which is, in fact, illusory. Speaking within the realms of chemistry for a moment – water itself is a simple element, its structure is not complex, yet what it achieves and the functions it performs play a central role supporting life on the planet. I believe that there is always elegance in simplicity and that a good negotiation strategy and the tactics utilised to implement it should always be as uncluttered as possible – the strategies deployed around the negotiation table should play a central role in supporting the life of the organisation – in ensuring its longevity, competitive success and advantage. This, after all, is why you are engaging in commercial negotiation: to reap rewards, to grow stronger, to achieve corporate success.

A further dimension to this strategy is that water is sometimes clear and sometimes it is opaque. The same could easily be said for the activities and possible outcomes around the negotiation table. Clarity equates to certainty, whilst opaqueness equates to uncertainty. Consider what you yourself are projecting or showing: on the table or hidden, both of which are relevant and are elements of the negotiation process. For me, the most inspirational and thought-provoking element of the Water Strategy is the inherent flexibility of water: it always follows the easiest route, but if it finds itself blocked, it flows around or over or under and continues on its way. The author would suggest very strongly that when it comes to sitting at the negotiation table, then you are capable of flowing in this way; that your strategy has flexibility and that it can change as much as needed. Earlier on, I had made the statement several times that there is no place for rigidity in commercial negotiation strategies and tactics, even if it means reaching the Exit Point and walking away. This is still another option at your disposal and you should never be so inflexible as to not consider implementing it should the situation dictate.

I hope that the reader will find 'The Water Strategy' as powerful and versatile as I have always done and that the powers of visualisation and analogy involved within it enhance your own personal approach to negotiations, whatever they may be.

I DON'T SPEAK YOUR LANGUAGE

This might well be the singular most common strategy that I've encountered when negotiating cross-culturally. As mentioned in 'The Water Strategy' above, there is always both elegance and effectiveness contained within simplicity. What could be simpler than to have a translator present who will manage the linguistic interface between the parties? Often, the most senior individual (i.e. the *de facto* decision maker) often doesn't speak (in my case) English or so it's claimed. I have looked across the table on many occasions and known that despite the poker face on the individual across from me, they understand what I'm saying perfectly. There are a number of dimensions to this approach, with the greatest advantage being the extra time provided whilst the translation is occurring. I once ensured that I had a native Arabic speaker on the team, an individual from Egypt but who spoke flawless English. We agreed from a tactical perspective that we wouldn't reveal that we knew that there was no need for a translator, nor that we had a fluent native speaker in our team who understood everything that they said. My team member told me that when the translator was translating, he was actually having a discussion with his boss; the translator was actually a sub-manager himself posing as a hired translator. So these guys were able to speak in private (or so they thought) at their leisure; they took their time to discuss amongst themselves everything that was said by us prior to retranslating. This proved to be a secret weapon for us. I was surprised that they spoke so openly about matters and issues pertinent and relevant to the negotiation at hand, so sure that we couldn't understand them. We would go over what had been said either at the breaks (if we had privacy) or in the evenings before the next day.

An additional caveat here – if you are going to use a translator, make sure that they are proficient in their skills and come from an unimpeachable source. I once hired a translator and was told at lunchtime by a member of the other negotiation team that he wasn't translating what I was saying and was actually giving quite a different 'spin' on my words. We discovered that he (the translator) actually worked for a competitor and was actively sabotaging the negotiation. He was arrested that night leaving the hotel, as when he was stopped his bags contained a lot of our paperwork and confidential information. Industrial espionage at its best!

CREDIBILITY THROUGH EXTERNAL VALIDATION

In the author's opinion, the simplest strategy of them all (and this can be used tactically too) is to have credibility through external validation. This may take many forms, from letters after a person's name to professional acknowledgement from their peers and/or industry that they are knowledgeable within their area of expertise. Everyone wants to be taken seriously around the table and external validation is often the simplest way of establishing validity, especially when dealing with unknown parties. Credibility also implies trust and believability in someone's expertise and competence. However, like so many things, if you are seeking credibility through external validation, you must be careful as validation in itself is also representative of a vast continuum. Consider, for example, how an MBA from one university might well be considered to be better than one from a lesser-known institution. Yet both qualifications are identical – it gets back to perception. As mentioned earlier, perception does not necessitate a state of truth, but it is often what matters the most to the perceiver. People utilise external validation all the time: going for job interviews, applying to study something, looking to join a club or organisation. However, a cautionary note here. Notwithstanding fraud and downright dishonesty, the external validation 'game' is very often 'smoke and mirrors' as individuals attempt to bend or stretch the truth to create a perception. An academic that I once had the misfortune to meet was a snob and a vainglorious individual who liked to brag about how well published he was. The problem, though, was that where he submitted his articles, no one was ever going to see them as they appeared in the equivalent of the 'Outer Mongolian Daily Blatt' or 'Yurt International' (both fictitious, in case you were wondering!), but you get the point. He was well published within his subject and was able to gain some external validation due to this by shaping perceptions. This type of external validation will not stand up to close inspection, but in truth, it is not often that it will be closely questioned or examined. People read the label on the box but don't inspect the contents.

THE 'TANGENTIAL PARADOX'

This strategy is about getting what you want, but getting it in a very convoluted manner, going off on a significant tangent. It's about being able to convince your counterparty that you are settling for less and giving them more than you'd like, whereas paradoxically you are getting precisely what you wanted at the very start (your optimum outcome). It is a very complex strategy and utilises practically everything contained in this book. I would suggest to you that it is an elite-level negotiator strategy but may be useful if this is you or may still be useful if this is where you aspire to be. No strategy is foolproof. As mentioned many times, ultimately the outcome of a negotiation is uncertain, BUT you can stack the deck as much as possible in your favour.

In order to execute the 'TP' strategy, you must have very good intelligence – information, facts and knowledge relevant to everything connected to the negotiation to come and the fulfilment of your strategy. In short, your due diligence process should be nothing short of superb. This is step 1.

Step 2 is to ensure that you propose your optimal outcome to the counterparties, knowing full well that they will either reject it outright or begin to offer compromises and alternative suggestions/positions. This is where you want to be – you will seem to have moved on and utilise the other alternatives and suggestions as further obfuscation – to appear engaged fully in seeking another alternative outcome.

In step 3, you will strongly play the role of 'Devil's Advocate' – probing, seeking and pointing out various weaknesses or unacceptable things from your perspective (remember though that there will always be an element of burn off; you must just choose the right time to offer something). During this step, you are actually also playing for time as through the DD process, you are aware of an event or something that is going to happen that is going to significantly weaken the counterparty's position. This is why the DD is crucial for this strategy to succeed. If this is not the case, then this strategy may not be the best one to adopt.

In step 4, the change that you anticipated or were waiting for occurs and you immediately capitalise by suggesting your original (or slightly modified) proposal, pointing out how this is now the best option moving forward for everyone. In reality, this might well be the case, and if events unfold to an even more beneficial level, you may actually have a significant level of power to seal the deal as it may hurt the counterparties more not to conclude matters with you. Furthermore, this is the stage in the negotiation process where you might utilise the burn off items in order to further achieve your aims.

Here's an example of this strategy in action:

You are a new market entrant and need a factory premises to run a production process. You've looked around the city and identified a number of sights. Through DD, you discover that several of the choicest ones in terms of location (proximity to clients/customers) and supporting infrastructure (roads/rail/harbour) are actually owned by the same people.

You propose the optimum location out of the possibilities, but you know that it is far too expensive for your fledgling organisation and that the owners are actually about to lease the premises to another organisation. They suggest a number of other sites, pushing hard on the one that they are the most desperate to shift. You seem to contemplate this option, but point out that the factory space would need to be configured and the loading bays and car parking facilities would need quite a bit of work. The offices are also shabby and would need to be redecorated. The counterparty says that they are happy to accept this expense in return for a five-year lease. This site is the worst out of all the possible options; the landlord had been unable to rent it out for the last several years. You also discover that this is a big drain on the owner as they still actually have a mortgage on it and it is making no money. A five-year lease on this premises is an absolute no go for your team. The process becomes protracted (deliberately by you) as you seem to be interested in the worst site, but also want to rethink about other sites. You are also having talks with other property owners. None of them have anything that interests you, but this is important as it makes your prime party uneasy and uncertain as to whether or not they are going to close a deal with you.

The price of steel rises sharply (this is what you were expecting to happen) and this makes the conversion works of the suggested site too expensive for the landlord. Also, the government raises the level of Corporation Tax (CT) and introduces new environmental levies for the disposal of waste. You had heard that these changes were also probable but were uncertain of the precise time frame, though intelligence seemed to suggest within the next six months (the CT raise everyone knew about, but the environmental policy was a shock to many but not you). The other organisation that was going to agree a lease with the prime site decides that they are going to relocate, as their business will be significantly affected by both the steel price and the new environmental regime, neither of which affect your business. You point out the new costs of overhauling the proposed site and suggest that as there is no real amount of conversion work required at the prime site the landlord would save a significant amount of money. As a gesture of good will (or so it seems), you suggest that you will take a seven-year lease on the prime site (it's absolutely perfect for your business). The owner counters (predictably) that they will grant the lease to your organisation if you would accept a 12-year lease. Your counteroffer is a ten-year lease (another thing that you wanted in the beginning) and that you would carry out required improvements (which are minor) at your own expense in exchange for the rental to be deferred and only to start four calendar months after the site is fully operational (this gives you a working capital window). The deal is signed and everyone is happy – and you achieved your optimal outcome.

As I hoped to have pointed out with example above, the 'TP' strategy is a good one, but also relatively high risk. You have to be reasonably confident when you discover facts and information that you can leverage in the negotiation are going to happen and within a practicable time frame to be of use in the negotiation process. Here's a thought for you – I have discovered in the course of my negotiation career that information is always there. It's just a question of looking for it – everyone hides things – and often being 'diligent' in your due diligence: paying attention, listening and being patient will always yield results.

Silver Bullet: The strategy selected and the tactics employed to realise it must always be chosen with the utmost care to align with both the negotiation at hand and the wider desires and objectives of the organisation (i.e. strategic fit). The negotiator must always examine the ramifications of the shorter-term actions and reactions against the longer-term implications and ramifications.

14

TEAM NEGOTIATIONS

Teams are interesting things to me. Some of them work well and some of them, well work – or seem to. I have often viewed the team environment as a microcosm of both the negotiation process and the wider world. Different people have different knowledge, views, skills, beliefs and opinions; yet, as part of a team, the trick here is to harness all this diversity towards a common goal. There are a number of problems associated with this seemingly straightforward statement. The biggest one involves people (I'm not joking!). The first issue we have discussed earlier in the book – that of 'self-interest,' the 'what's in it for me' syndrome. Sometimes, this is anathema to the success of any team, as in my opinion, a collective identity must be forged. The individuals must become a part of the whole, the components of the team itself. Teams that tend to perform and achieve goals (I have seen this countless times from the Project Management perspective) are those that become something more than the people in them. This collective identity supersedes the individual identity. Individuals become proud and engaged to be part of the team. There is a cautionary note here. Some teams can develop an elitist opinion of themselves and get to a stage where they feel that they are no longer accountable to others: that they know best and that they can become 'exclusive and conclusive' about themselves, arrogant with their own success. Another negative of this is that if you disband a high performing team (results for the organisation discounted), individuals who join another team might not integrate as they believe that they are better than their co-workers. They can cause conflict and tension and significantly impede the progress or results of the subsequent new team.

DOI: 10.4324/9781003263722-14

Negotiation is interesting from the perspective that it can be either a 'Lone Wolf' activity (the 'Solo' negotiator) or, as is very common with larger, more complex scenarios, a team endeavour. They are different beasts indeed, but the reason I make this statement is for the reader to understand that care must be ensured when attempting to mix a solo operator into a team environment. Often, it won't work and needs some pre-thought when deciding the composition of a negotiation team. Most Lone Wolfs prefer to operate alone. They don't want to be part of a pack. Logically, the team approach to a negotiation works best when multiple skillsets are required and a wider spread of specialist knowledge (consider comments in the previous chapter regarding the Specialist Team approach to negotiating) is able to address specificity of technical/financial/operational issues. In my opinion, the single greatest determinant of the success or failure of a negotiation team hinges around who is the team leader. As mentioned earlier in the book, there must be someone in charge – the conductor of the orchestra, the captain of the ship. Often, the ability to control and co-ordinate different people and their abilities is the singular most daunting aspect of the negotiation. In the author's opinion, the essence of good leadership of a negotiation team is to know your people and be able to match them to the role that best suits them. Some members of the team might be more comfortable operating in the background – performing due diligence – making sure the team admin is up to date and other such similar tasks and duties. Others might want a seat on the firing line, to be in the 'thick of the action,' to feel challenged and excel, to operate outside of their comfort zone, whilst other team members might want a bit of both. There are a number of significant advantages to operating as part of a negotiation team. For many people, dealing with uncertainty moves them firmly out of their 'comfort zone,' which is not a place they desire to be. Being part of a team is automatically confidence inspiring as you are not alone and can share your thoughts and feelings with others in the team, ask for help and (if need be) find reassurance that you are performing your role correctly. If a team is operating with efficiency and everyone is playing their part, it becomes much easier for the team to be able to form a clear picture of the current status of the negotiation at hand. Collectively, the team can review and offer personal insights and opinions and contribute towards any corrective actions that might be required if it is felt that the process is going off-track – more 'eyes' on a problem – making the solution easier to find (in some circumstances, but not all), as there is a 'collective' problem-solving ability and a greater depth of perception. If there is a diverse range of specialist knowledge within the team, then the possibility of something arising that catches everyone by surprise is largely mitigated. This is another reason why the Japanese favour this approach. As mentioned earlier, a strong, competent and organised professional negotiation team presents a strong identity to the counterparties. This can often portray your organisation as competent and an efficient 'well-oiled' machine where all the working parts are functioning optimally.

As surely as there are advantages to operating within a team around the negotiation table, there are also a number of disadvantages that must not be taken lightly. This is why the assessment of the Lone Wolf versus the Team approach should always be contemplated carefully. I have already alluded to the phenomenon called 'group think,' where the team begins to believe that it is the best and no longer subject to the same rules as everyone else. It becomes elitist to the point of excluding anyone else or any advice/guidance from other parties, regardless of who they may be. Another of the serious disadvantages of negotiation teams is when what I call the 'Teflon Shoulder Pad' syndrome manifests. No one wants to be the individual who says 'I think we should…,' so decisions made become a 'management by consensus'. The decision-making process becomes turgid and confused as there may be a lack of agreement on issues. The biggest danger of this manifestation is that it evolves into a state where there is no longer any clear accountability or ownership amongst the team. These factors in themselves can create a much higher stress level among individuals, whilst simultaneously creating a much higher potential for internal conflict to arise. Obviously, this is not a state conducive to conducting a focussed and professional negotiation.

Silver Bullet: The keys to effective team-based negotiations:

1. **Someone undisputedly in charge**
2. **Delegation**
3. **Accountability**
4. **Ownership**
5. **Effective reporting and information sharing**

6 **Collective input – some decision-making**
7 **Clear roles of team members**
8 **Review mechanisms**

REMOTE/VIRTUAL TEAMS

Pre-COVID, the 'virtual' or 'remote' team was on the rise as it had a number of advantages inherent to itself. COVID-19 changed the world to a degree that at one point, nearly all interactions between people became conducted on a remote basis, and it seemed to work. People who had never met began to do business with one another and individuals who may be geographically dispersed around the world could form competent teams to carry out tasks (given too that there wasn't any other option). However, in my opinion, these 'teams' will never 'form' or operate in the same manner as a 'live' team, simply because they lack the face-to-face 'human dynamic'; you are never going to get to really know the talking head in the corner of your computer screen. Humans are fundamentally social creatures who will often begin to bond with one another during social activities, where people can relax and get to know each other better by not simply focussing on work-related matters. The reader may recall that in an earlier chapter, I explained how people immediately began to size each other up when they first meet; this is much harder to do virtually (if not impossible) compared to being face-to-face with the counterparties. I would also state that many of the subtle nuances that the negotiator is trained to watch for could be missed. Although they work, and we will discuss their advantages shortly, I always prefer to conduct my negotiation business live as opposed to virtual from the perspective of nearly everything that I have said in this book. The main reason for this is that often they suffer from integration problems and issues; people in different time zones, cross-cultural interactions and feelings of isolation often come to the fore within the virtual team environment and this significantly affects the output from the team compared to a tight, dynamic, live team. The virtual team also raises questions about effective control. It is very difficult if you are in New York to be absolutely certain how much time your colleague is spending on their role if they are in Perth, Australia, and it is possible that a team member is or becomes disinterested or unmotivated. I believe that the virtual environment can amplify the scope for misunderstandings between people, as I refer back to the 'talking head' on a screen – you don't know this individual and might mistake their facial expression or tone of voice. This is the only information you've got to work with. The relationship angle is severely diminished. The author is of the opinion that this further exacerbates the potential for cross-cultural misunderstandings to take root and flourish. Indeed, in my experience, some cultures place an exceedingly high importance on personal interactions and relationship building. Of course, we have all had to adjust to the changed world that we now find ourselves in, but I foresee that the virtual operation will often be a 'mixer.' Certain elements of a negotiation might be conducted virtually for operational reasons, whilst the highest stake, commercially sensitive issues will probably continue to be negotiated face to face.

The advantages of remote or virtual teams are of course quite significant. People don't have to travel. So from an expense perspective immediately, costs are significantly slashed. The team can assemble immediately when called upon by simply connecting and joining the meeting. As the virtual team has the ability to reach everyone everywhere, the access to expertise is far wider. I believe that one of the strongest points in favour of this medium is that team members, particularly if they are geographically dispersed, could be busy 24 hours a day collectively, working on a project or preparing for a negotiation.

Whether a live or a virtual negotiation is occurring, one of the key attributes that the modern negotiator must have is to be culturally sensitive and knowledgeable about the counterparties' accepted norms and beliefs and how they establish the behaviour that is to be expected during business activities as well as any cultural implications for members of your own team. Quite simply, people from different cultures operate and behave in different ways. Securing the requisite cultural knowledge prior to initiation should always be part of any due diligence process that you carry out. Different nationalities have different proximal distances that they use: different patterns of speech where some are circumspect and some are blunt, possibly to the point of rudeness, but the rudeness is not meant. It is just that particular cultural approach. I could fill a complete separate book about the mistakes that are made by not understanding cultural norms, some of which have ended proceedings then and there. Some cultures speak more and some listen more. Some are (as mentioned above) very direct whilst others are circuitous, some are very passionate and emotional whilst others may be very cold, unemotional and in control. During the course of your negotiation career, I am certain that you will encounter all of these traits and foibles. Remember to be informed and knowledgeable about what is expected of you. Often, by showing cultural knowledge in terms of manners, the counterparty is more open to dealing with you, recognising that you have taken the time and trouble to learn something about where they come from, their habits and customs. This knowledge will never be of a detriment to you – I assure you!

I once led a negotiation team of five in a complex deal. We were dealing with people from the Middle East and they fielded a team of ten at the table, a lot of whom were very senior people. There were three very experienced people in my team and two who were mid-level in experience. As I have hoped to share with you throughout this book (and particularly in the previous chapter), there is always room for the unexpected to happen. So, this negotiation got off to a good start and everyone seemed to be getting along. After lunch, I was very surprised by how knowledgeable the other gentlemen appeared to be as to our position on various items to be discussed. This continued the following day, with most of my team commenting on it. Anyway, to cut a long story short, we had a traitor in our team. One of my own people, who admittedly I didn't know well, but he was forced upon us as a liaison, really took the liaison role seriously. He was reporting to the counterparty everything that we discussed in private, either during breaks or in the evenings. He did us incredible damage. I insisted he be removed and the Middle East party was not happy. We eventually (about four days later) reached an agreement, but I often wonder to myself from time to time if there might have been a better outcome (it was a fair settlement) had we not had the skulduggery in the first place. Always be prepared for anything to happen around the negotiation table.

I hope that you, the reader, have enjoyed this book and that you have gained some new knowledge, insights and ideas that you can implement into your own strategies and tactics when negotiating. I wish you every success with your future endeavours and who knows, perhaps one of these days we might well find ourselves sitting opposite or alongside one another around a table! If it ever happens, I will look forward to that day. The best of luck to you all.

INDEX

Note: *Italic* page numbers refer to figures.

For Product Safety Concerns and Information please contact our EU representative GPSR@taylorandfrancis.com
Taylor & Francis Verlag GmbH, Kaufingerstraße 24, 80331 München, Germany

www.ingramcontent.com/pod-product-compliance
Lightning Source LLC
LaVergne TN
LVHW021131300926
849160LV00010B/965
* 9 7 8 1 0 3 2 2 0 4 7 5 8 *